# The
# Beach

**Queen Anne** (1665-1714)

This portrait of Anne, Queen of Great Britain, is attributed to the school of Sir Godfrey Kneller and was painted circa 1710. It features Queen Anne in her coronation robe. The modern day city of Virginia Beach was formed in 1963 from the merger of Princess Anne County (named for her when she was Princess Anne) and the City of Virginia Beach.

# The
# Beach

---

## A History of Virginia Beach, Virginia

Revised Edition

### The Virginia Beach Public Library

1996

Based on the 1976 first edition written by
Kathleen M. Eighmey

*Cataloging-in-Publication Data*

Virginia Beach Public Library.
  The beach: a history of Virginia Beach, Virginia / Virginia Beach Public Library.
    p.  cm.
  Library of Congress Catalog Card No.: 95-83434
  ISBN  0-9653325-0-0
  1. Virginia Beach (Va.) -- History.     I. Title

  975.551

Cover design and layout by Frank Smith
Cover photo by H.C. Mann, courtesy of the Norfolk Public Library

# Contents

Based on the original text by Kathleen M. Eighmey

# Reference Map

Many names used in this book refer to places known to local residents but which may not be familiar to others. This reference map gives the reader a basic reference to the geography of Virginia Beach and the major places mentioned in the text.

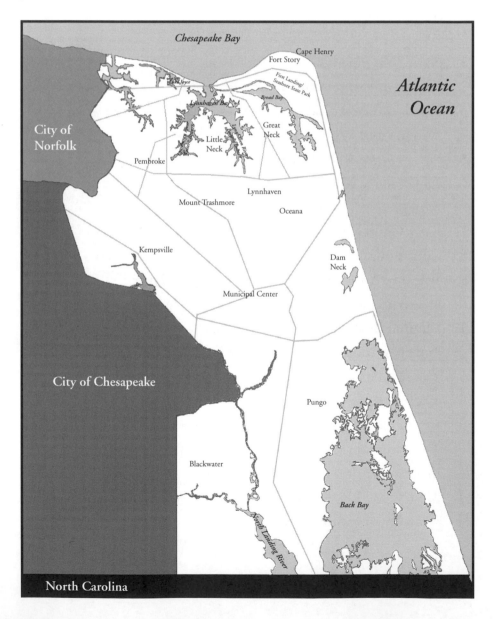

# Illustrations

# *Acknowledgments*

It would be an impossible task to give proper acknowledgment to all who generously assisted in the preparation of *The Beach*. However, special appreciation must be expressed to the following:

Kathleen M. Eighmcy, the author of the first edition of *The Beach,* whose original book provided the framework for the four writers of the revised edition

Individuals and institutions who verified information, provided expertise, and suggested new paths of research:

The Association for the Preservation of Virginia Antiquities
The Casemate Museum, Fort Monroe
Mark Reed and Vicki Harvey, Francis Land House
The Hampton Roads Naval Museum, Norfolk
Kirn Memorial Library, Norfolk
The Library of Virginia, Richmond
Marilyn Melchor, APVA, for Lynnhaven House
The Reverend Larry Stanwyck Hinton, Mount Zion A.M.E. Church
Fielding Tyler, The Old Coast Guard Station
St. Mark A.M.E. Church
Roberta Whisman, Thoroughgood House
Stephen Mansfield for Upper Wolfsnare
Clarence Warnstaff and Thomas Leahy, Department of Public
    Utilities, City of Virginia Beach
Georgia Christie,Virginia Beach City Public Schools
Tom Carr, Virginia Department of Conservation and Recreation

Others who helped find or provided illustrations:
Edgar T. Brown
Elizabeth Evans of Campbell, Barker and Farley
Irene Roughton, Chrysler Museum of Art
Eastern Shore Chapel
Debby Padgett, Jamestown Settlement
Claudia McFall, Mariners' Museum
Public Affairs Office, Naval Air Station Oceana

Peggy Haile, Sargeant Memorial Room, Norfolk Public Library
Julie Pouliot, The Old Coast Guard Station
W. "Rip" Rylance
Charles Sibley
Louis Cullipher, Agriculture Department, City of Virginia Beach
Michael Davy and J. Curtis Fruit, Circuit Court Clerk's Office, City
     of Virginia Beach
Pat Hamm, Convention and Visitor Development, City of Virginia
     Beach
Carole Arnold, Public Information Office, City of Virginia Beach
The *Virginian-Pilot*
Keith Egloff, Virginia Department of Historic Resources

Carolyn Barkley, who began the revision of the early chapters in the late
eighties and who provided encouragement during the later revision process

Patrick Brennan, Semmes Chapman, Ed Fraim, Melinda Lukei, Stephen
Mansfield, Mac Rawls, Mark Reed, Helen Rountree, and the late Floyd
Painter, who offered suggestions for the early revision to Carolyn Barkley

The Friends of the Virginia Beach Public Library, whose continuing
efforts enable the library to provide enriching activities to the community

The City Council and City Manager, who advanced us the funds to
publish *The Beach* and Martha J. Sims, Director of the Department of
Public Libraries, who supports a workplace environment which fosters
creative endeavors

And finally to *The Beach* Team:

Toni Lohman, who provided leadership and unruffled attention
throughout the revision process

Writers Martha Lewis Taylor, Dotsy Harland, Mary Lovell Swetnam, and
Theresa Dunleavy, who studied hundreds of pages of research material,
devoted many hours to the revision, and created this edition

Researchers Mary Lovell Swetnam, Dorothy Williams, Katherine St.
James, Dee Dallman, Theresa Dunleavy, C. Michelle Norton, Diane
Wetterlin, and former staff member Janet Forbes, who tracked down
elusive details and verified innumerable facts

Cheryl Gayton, who managed the workflow, tracked chapters, and organized a myriad of ever-changing details

Frank Smith, Susan Zwick, Donna Gant, and Jackie Lewis, who examined hundreds of photographs, drawings, and maps, then selected the illustrations for this edition

Copy editors Judy Pate, Barbara Granger, and Amy Belcher, who offered valuable suggestions and who held us strictly to the standards of the *Chicago Manual of Style*

Sean O'Connell, Aleene Wicher, Dawn Chabrol, and Donna Gant who created the index and prepared the bibliography

The Central Library Microcomputer Room technicians, who served as a computer resource for the writers

Typists Sandra Francis and Jeff McCreary, who patiently deciphered several drafts

Hillary Burns and Dorothy Williams, who proof-read the final draft

Frank Smith, who designed the layout of the book

Nancy Miller, Frank Smith, and Susan Paddock, who took care of the detailed business procedures necessary for publishing the book

Jeanette Friedman, who registered the book with the Library of Congress and obtained the copyright and the ISBN

Bonnie Mathews, Theresa Dunleavy, Cindy Hart, and Marcia Hart, who combined their enthusiasm with keen advertising skills to market the book

Pam Harris, Mary Lawrence, and Doris Brownley, who managed the business of getting the finished book to the readers

The Information Services staff of the Central Library, who spent time researching and verifying information, and their supervisor Pat Cook, who made it possible for the staff to get the work done

And especially to the library staff in all agencies, who assumed the duties of team members so their time could be devoted to completing the book.

# Introduction

L ibrarians hesitate to admit they cannot find information, particularly about the history of their own city. This edition of *The Beach* was written because material on the history of Virginia Beach was hard to locate. It was scattered and difficult to use, especially by the students who come to the library every year working on local history projects. An earlier edition of *The Beach*, published in 1976, was long out of print, and some of the details it contained were no longer accurate.

The Department of Public Library's Local History Committee wrestled for several years with the need for an updated book on Virginia Beach history. In 1995 a team of library staff was formed to completely rewrite and publish a new edition of *The Beach*. Creating a book was a total role reversal for librarians, who were accustomed to using and buying books, not writing and publishing them. This has proven to be a valuable experience, however, giving all those involved a new appreciation for the authors and publishers who create the materials used everyday by library staff.

We hope *The Beach* will provide a glimpse into our past, of the "white hilly sand like unto the Downes, and along the shores great plentie of Pines and Firres," as Captain John Smith described Cape Henry in 1607. As the City prepares for the twenty-first century, we also hope that this view of how Virginia Beach came to be will help guide our steps into the future.

Toni Lohman
*The Beach* Team Leader

# Chapter 1

# *Native Virginians*

European explorers and colonists were not the first people to set foot on Virginia's soil. Archaeological evidence indicates that small bands of nomadic hunters had roamed the area for thousands of years prior to the first European encounters with Native Americans. During the Paleo-Indian period which ended in 8000 B.C.,[1] local land forms may have been quite different from the present topography of Virginia Beach.

Floyd Painter, a local archaeologist, described the ancient Great Neck area as having the highest elevation in lower Tidewater, approximately 200 feet above sea level. The Chesapeake Bay did not exist except as a broad valley through which the Susquehanna River flowed. The Atlantic shore may have been as much as ninety miles away. Paleo-Indian artifacts have been found in the Great Neck, Seashore State Park (now First Landing/ Seashore State Park), and Bayville Farms areas.[2] Archaeologist James G. Pritchard reported uncovering Paleo-Indian fluted point tips, scrapers, and gravers from excavations at the Quail Spring site in the Great Neck area of Virginia Beach.[3]

The climate changed, glacial ice sheets melted, and Paleo-Indian people adapted to their changing environment. As nomadic existence gave way to the use of seasonal habitation sites, the Paleo-Indian period was succeeded by the Archaic period, which dated from approximately 8000 B.C. to 500 B.C. Archaic people left evidence that they revisited their former campsites yearly or seasonally. They hunted, fished, and gathered plants and shellfish. Archaic inhabitants worked with polished stone tools and hunted with a throwing stick which gave a spear more force. A bannerstone, which was a ground and perforated stone, was attached and may have been used for weight, balance, or supernatural reasons. Bannerstones have been found at Back Bay, Dam Neck, Lynnhaven Inlet, and Kempsville.[4]

Archaic people used pots carved out of soapstone. Scientists have used a nuclear reactor and neutron activation analysis to test samples of soapstone in Virginia quarries and compare them with samples taken from prehistoric Indian artifacts and pots. Analysis of the soapstone shows that trading patterns of the tribes were geographical and were specific to language groups. The Chula quarry in Amelia County appears to have been the source of soapstone for most of the Algonquian-speaking Indians, while the Siouan groups used quarries in Albemarle and Nelson counties.[5]

The term Woodland period categorizes the native people who lived from approximately 1000 B.C. to the European contact period.[6] During this period the native population increased and village sites became more permanent. Villages were usually located along rivers and creeks as they were the main routes of transportation and communication. Food gathering and agriculture took precedence over hunting. Indian corn, tobacco, pumpkins, and beans were cultivated. Use of the bow and arrow developed during the Woodland period. In addition to carved bowls, fabric impressed pottery was produced.[7] The Long Creek Midden in the Great Neck area is an extensive Woodland occupation site.[8]

When Europeans first began exploring the Chesapeake Bay area, Virginia was inhabited by Indians of three linguistic stocks: Iroquoian, Siouan, and Algonquian. The Iroquoian Indians (Nottoway and Meherrin) lived on the south side of the James River. The Siouan tribes (Monacan and Mannahoac) inhabited the area west of the Fall line (the zone typified by river rapids which occur where ground descends from the higher Piedmont elevations to the lower Tidewater areas). The Algonquian tribes occupied the Tidewater area of Virginia as well as the two Eastern Shore counties of Accomack and Northampton. The Pamlico and Chowanoc peoples, also Algonquian speakers, lived on the Virginia-North Carolina border.

The Chesapeakes, one of the Algonquian tribes, occupied the land from the Atlantic Ocean to the Elizabeth River. They spoke the Powhatan dialect of the Algonquian language but had resisted joining Powhatan's chiefdom. Powhatan was an Indian chief, who, before the coming of the colonists, had achieved political dominance over more than thirty Tidewater Algonquian speaking tribes (estimated to have been as few as 14,000 by some experts and as many as 30,000 by others). Powhatan had inherited six of these tribes—the Powhatan, Arohatock, Appamattuck, Pamunkey, Youghtanund, and Mattaponi. The additional groups were conquered or coerced into joining Powhatan.[9]

The Chesapeakes lived in towns which were named and had boundaries but which might not be inhabited during all of the seasons. Their lodges were built of saplings set in the ground in rectangular fashion, bent and

**Longhouse,** scarecrow platform, and garden as recreated at Jamestown Indian Village, Jamestown Settlement, Williamsburg, Virginia *above*

Courtesy of Jamestown Settlement

**Virginia Beach Excavation Site,** showing original longhouse postholes, circa A.D. 1400 to A.D. 1600
The site was located in a residential neighborhood on Pungo Ridge, north of Great Neck Road. The longhouse on the "Great Neck Site" measured 31 feet long by 16 feet wide. *below*

Courtesy of the Virginia Department of Historic Resources

tied together at the top, and covered with bark or mats of reeds and grasses. These mats provided protection from cold winter winds but could be rolled up to provide ventilation in the summer months. There was a fire pit in the center of the floor and a smoke hole in the roof. A wide shelf around the interior was used for sitting and sleeping. The mats and skins used as bedding could be removed in the daytime and stored. The mats on the houses and the ones used as bedding also had the advantage of being portable, making village movement possible.[10]

The lodges were usually a short distance apart and were surrounded by garden plots and fields. The men cleared the fields, and the women planted crops of corn, pumpkins, squash, beans, and tobacco from April to June. They harvested the crops between August and October. The Indians supplemented their winter diet by hunting, gathering, and fishing.

Hunting, by groups or alone, was the men's responsibility. Entire villages would remove to the hunting grounds where deer were captured by various methods. At times, a group of Indian men would form a circle around the deer. The men then set fires around the perimeter of the circle in order to contain the deer. While the deer ran around the circle seeking a way out, the hunters would shoot them with bows and arrows. A slightly different variation occurred near rivers. Some hunters would herd the deer toward the river, while others waited in canoes to kill the animals as they swam into the water. At other times, individual hunters would dress in deer skin and antlers and would mimick deer behavior while stalking a deer. When the animal had been wounded by an arrow, the Indian would chase it down until it died. Trapping methods were used for smaller game such as beaver and otter.[11]

From late March until May, fishing supplied much of the Indians' diet. Fishing with poles, line, bait, and fishhooks has remained a recognizable method from the time period. However, Indian fishermen would at times leap into the water and swim with the hooked fish until it tired, in order to avoid losing the fish. Fish nets, fish traps, and weirs were used to catch migrating schools of fish. Although there is no archaeological evidence of the design of the weirs, European drawings show that the ones currently in use in the area are much like those used by the Powhatan Indians.[12]

The Chesapeakes supplemented their diet by gathering berries, edible roots, bird eggs, and shellfish. Oysters, clams, and mussels were also important food sources during the late spring and summer.

Although the Chesapeakes were at one time a relatively large tribe, Captain John Smith estimated the tribe had only 100 warriors in 1607.[13] Near the time that the Jamestown colonists arrived, Powhatan waged a war against the Chesapeakes. Powhatan's priests had prophesied that a nation would rise from the Chesapeake Bay and end his rule. Since the

Chesapeakes were the largest tribe on the bay itself, Powhatan assumed that the prophecy referred to them, and he attempted to annihilate them. Through stealth and treachery, he succeeded in killing all the warriors of the tribe, sparing only the women, children, and the royal family. The women and children were sent to live among tribes more loyal to Powhatan, mostly in the York River area. Only the royal or ruling family was allowed to stay in the traditional Chesapeake tribal area. Families loyal to Powhatan were sent to replace the dead and deported Chesapeakes. The new families were made subjects of the old Chesapeake royal family and thus were considered Chesapeakes. These new people may be the ones encountered by John Smith and the other English colonists.[14]

Although full-blooded Chesapeakes are no more, Chesapeake blood may still flow in their Native American, Black, and White descendants. Their name lives on in the great Chesapeake Bay and in such regional names as the present day city of Chesapeake (to the west of Virginia Beach) and Chesopeian Colony, a residential area in Virginia Beach.

## *Notes for Chapter 1*

1. Duane Champagne, ed., *The Native North American Almanac* (Detroit: Gale Research, Inc., 1994), 3.

2. Floyd Painter, "The Ancient Indian Town of Chesapeake on the Peninsula of Great Neck," *The Chesopiean* 17, August-October 1979, 65.

3. James G. Pritchard, "Quail Spring Paleo Occupation Site," *The Chesopiean* 3, June 1964, 60-61.

4. Ben C. McCary, "Bannerstones from the Dismal Swamp Area and Nearby Counties of Virginia and North Carolina," *Quarterly Bulletin, The Archeological Society of Virginia* 30, September 1975, 36.

5. Beverly Orndorff, "Indian Trading Traced By U.Va. Reactor," *Richmond* (Va) *Times Dispatch*, 12 January 1975, section A, 1.

6. Champagne, 3.

7. Ben C. McCary, *Indians in Seventeenth-Century Virginia* (Charlottesville, Va.: University Press of Virginia, 1957), 93.

8. Edward Jelks, ed. *Historical Dictionary of North American Archeology* (New York: Greenwood Press, 1988), 190.

9. Helen Rountree, *Pocahontas's People: The Powhatan Indians of Virginia through Four Centuries* (Norman, Ok.: University of Oklahoma Press, 1990), 25.

10. Helen Rountree, *The Powhatan Indians of Virginia: Their Traditional Culture* (Norman, Ok.: University of Oklahoma Press, 1989), 60-62.

11. Ibid., 39-40.

12. Ibid., 34-35.

13. Patrick H. Garrow, "An Ethnohistorical Study of the Powhatan Tribes," *The Chesopiean* 12, February-April 1974, 42.

14. Painter, 70-71.

# Chapter 2

# European Exploration and Settlement

I t is possible, even probable, that European explorers visited the Chesapeake Bay area now called Virginia Beach many years prior to the landing of the Jamestown settlers. There has been a persistent belief that Captain John Cabot may have visited the area in 1498.[1]  However, general sources on exploration which mention this notion consider it unlikely.[2]  It is also possible that Giovanni da Verazzano sailed past the Virginia Capes in 1524.  Additionally, there is documentation that in 1546 an English ship rode out a storm in a bay located at the thirty-seventh parallel.  This parallel runs through the mouth of the Chesapeake Bay.[3]

In 1570 an expedition of Jesuit priests, a novice, and an Indian guide arrived in Tidewater Virginia and sailed up the James River.  They landed on September 10 near what would become Jamestown.  The complete tale of this Spanish mission has little impact on the history of Princess Anne County and Virginia Beach, but it helps to illustrate that Europeans were not completely unknown in the area at the time when the "First Landing" occurred.[4]

On April 26, 1607, the vessels *Sarah Constant, Godspeed*, and *Discovery* arrived in Virginia with 104 Englishmen aboard.  Captain George Percy wrote the following account of the landing:

> *The six and twentieth day of April, about four o'clock in the morning, we descried the land of Virginia. . . . The same day we entered into the Bay of Ches-u-pi-oc directly, without any let or hinderance.  There we landed and discovered a little way, but we could find nothing worth the speaking of, but fair meadows and goodly tall trees, with such fresh waters running through the woods as I was almost ravished at the first sight thereof.*[5]

This first landing consisted of twenty-eight men who disembarked near what is now Cape Henry.  During the night they were attacked by Chesapeake Indians.  Captain Gabriel Archer and Mathew Morton, a sailor, were wounded.  As the Indians disappeared into the woods, the Englishmen retreated to their ships.

On the second day, another party went ashore and penetrated about eight miles inland without encountering any Indian settlements.  This landing was probably east of Lynnhaven Bay (called Morton's Bay after their wounded comrade), as the Chesapeake's principal town was located near the mouth of the Lynnhaven River.  Although no Indians were found, the Englishmen did find a fire where oysters were being roasted.  The Indians had fled, or at least withdrawn, leaving the oysters in the fire.  According to Captain Percy, "We ate some of the oysters which were very large and delicate in taste."[6]  These oysters became known as Lynnhaven oysters and enjoyed an international reputation as delicacies into the twentieth century.

On the third day, April 28, 1607, the Englishmen assembled and launched the shallop which they had brought with them.  This boat enabled Captain Christopher Newport to take a party northwest on the body of water known, by 1610, as Hampton Roads.  Near the present site of Hampton, they saw a forty-five foot Indian dugout log canoe.  Inland they reported finding "beautiful strawberries, four times bigger and better than ours in England."[7]

They returned to their anchorage that night, and the following day, April 29, they "set up a cross at Chesapeake Bay, and named that place Cape Henry"[8] in honor of King James's son, Henry Prince of Wales, who was next in line to the throne.  Cape Charles, across the bay, was named at the same time for Prince Charles who later became King Charles I, as his brother Henry predeceased their father, King James.  Captain John Smith later claimed to have named the headlands himself.  However, that is unlikely, as he was under arrest for suspicion of mutiny at the time of his arrival in Virginia.[9]  The names were chosen to honor the patron of the expedition and his family and to insure their continued interest in colonial pursuits.

In 1935 a large stone cross was erected amidst the sand dunes at Cape Henry to commemorate the first landing of the adventurers who went on to establish the first permanent English settlement in the New World at Jamestown on May 13, 1607.  The landing cross is the site of an annual celebration and pilgrimage conducted by The Order of Cape Henry, 1607 on the Sunday nearest to April 26.

One might wonder why it took so long to settle the area around the first landing site.  According to William Strachey (1572-1621), the settlement was not made at Cape Henry or Old Point Comfort (Fort Monroe),

Stephen Reid. ***The Landing at Cape Henry–April 1607***
1928. Oil on canvas, 50" x 62".

Courtesy of the Chrysler Museum of Art, Norfolk, Virginia
Gift of the Organizations and Citizens of Norfolk and vicinity in memory of
Alethea Serpell, past President, Council of Assembly Tidewater Women

because Captain Newport thought that those areas were too exposed. Additionally, the Council (in London) advised that they settle well up into the county, even as much as 100 miles, in order to avoid an attack by the Spanish. The first settlers brought few material possessions with them. They did, however, bring the English systems of law, local administration, and religion to colonial Virginia.[10]

Once the colony was established, land was granted or patented to adventurers to be settled and civilized. Headrights (land grants consisting of 100 acres per person for arrivals prior to 1616) were given to planters for each person they agreed to transport to Virginia. Because of these patents, the population of colonial Virginia developed into widely separated, self-sufficient, feudal-style manors.

In 1634 what began as plantations, hundreds, or corporations were grouped into larger administrative units called shires. The first Virginia shires (or counties) formed were Accawmack, Charles City, Henrico, James City, Warrosquyoake, Charles River, Elizabeth Citty, and Warwick River.[11] The total population of these counties in 1634 was 4,914 people. The area that was to become Princess Anne County was initially part of Elizabeth City (or Citty) County. At its formation in 1634, Elizabeth City extended to both sides of Hampton Roads and contained 1,670 people. Three years later, in 1637, the portion of Elizabeth City County lying south of Hampton Roads became New Norfolk County. The following year it, in turn, was divided into Upper and Lower Norfolk counties.[12]

Princess Anne County was formed from the eastern section of Lower Norfolk in 1691.[13] A small part of the Lynnhaven Parish boundary was erroneously left in Lower Norfolk County until four years later. An act of the assembly of 1695 made Princess Anne County coterminous with the Lynnhaven Parish boundaries as established in 1642.[14]

Princess Anne County was named for Anne, the younger daughter of James II and Anne Hyde. When King James (II of England and VII of Scotland) was deposed during the "Glorious Revolution" in 1688, his other daughter Mary and her husband, William of Orange, gained the throne. Anne, a staunch Protestant, sided with William in 1688 and became Queen of England upon his death in 1702. Copies of the document which proclaimed Anne Queen of England, Scotland, France, Ireland, and the Colony Dominion and plantation of Virginia are to be found in various local history sources. The text and punctuation of these documents vary depending on the transcriber. Handwritten and transcribed texts are available on microform but are difficult to read.

Princess Anne County had a continuous shore line from the North Carolina-Virginia border, along the Atlantic coast to Cape Henry, and west along the Chesapeake Bay shore to Little Creek Inlet. One look at the map of the area makes it evident that water was to play an important part in the history of the county. The map is honeycombed with bays, rivers, creeks, and lakes which reach deep into the county. There were, and still are, very few places which are not near water or without easy access to it. Since water was the colonial means of transportation and communication, nearly every settler had a skiff or shallop for market, church, business, or social activities.

While we consider the Virginia Beach land and water forms we see today to be the same as they were in 1607, it is evident from old maps that several water courses have changed. For instance, a 1673 map by Augustin Herrman (located in the Library of Congress) shows the inlet for Lynnhaven at Pleasure House Creek about two miles west of the present site. The present location of the inlet is attributed to local fishermen who desired to shorten the circuitous route from the Lynnhaven to their Chesapeake Bay fishing grounds. One source states that Adam

Keeling, Esq. "caused a dike to be cut across from the two nearest or most convenient points on the neighboring shores of the river and bay."[15] The tidal currents gradually eroded the small channel into what is now Lynnhaven Inlet.

Between Cape Henry and Rudee Inlet there is evidence of another, now nonexistent, inlet. A 1695 map of the area (which Sadie Scott Kellam and V. Hope Kellam located in the Library of Congress) indicates that the entire northeast corner of Cape Henry was cut off from the rest of the county by "a continuous water route from Chesapeake Bay in Lynnhaven River, out Long Creek (. . . 'sometimes called Stratton's') into Broad Bay (Battses Bay), into Linkhorn (Lincolne) Bay to Little Neck Creek, or perhaps Chrystal Lake, to the Ocean."[16] The maps of the Spanish Jesuit expedition, which explored the Chesapeake Bay in the early fall of 1570, also indicate an inlet near Crystal Lake.[17]

At Lake Tecumseh, now known as Brinson Inlet Lake (per a Virginia Beach Council Resolution dated June 16, 1986), and at Back Bay there are also geophysical indications of harbor inlets. Coastal storms may have changed all of these landmarks just as they continue to change our modern coastline. These waterways throughout the county afforded protection from the sea, provided a means of transportation and communication, and tied the fertile land together.

## *Notes for Chapter 2*

1. Florence Kimberly Turner, *Gateway to the New World: A History of Princess Anne County, Virginia 1607-1824* (Easley, S.C.: Southern Historical Press, 1984), 18.

2. Carl Waldman and Alan Wexler, *Who Was Who in World Exploration* (New York: Facts on File, 1992), 110-111.

3. Helen Rountree, *Pocahontas's People: The Powhatan Indians of Virginia through Four Centuries* (Norman, Ok.: University of Oklahoma Press, 1990), 15.

4. Ibid., 16.

5. Conway Whittle Sams, *The Conquest of Virginia: The Second Attempt* (Norfolk, Va.: Keyser-Doherty Printing Corp., 1929), 107.

6. Ibid., 127.

7. Ibid., 129.

8. Ibid., 130.

9. Ibid., 94-95.

10. Ibid., 140.

11. Morgan Poitiaux Robinson, "Virginia Counties: Those Resulting from Virginia Legislation," *Bulletin of the Virginia State Library* 9, nos.1, 2, 3, January, April, July, 1916, 36.

12. Ibid., 165.

13. William Waller Hening, ed., *The Statutes at Large; Being a Collection of All the Laws of Virginia, from the First Session of the Legislature in the Year 1619* (1819-23; reprint, Charlottesville, Va.: University of Virginia Press for the Jamestown Foundation of the Commonwealth of Virginia, 1969), 95.

14. Ibid., 128.

15. William S. Forrest, *Historical and Descriptive Sketches of Norfolk and Vicinity: Including Portsmouth and the Adjacent Counties, During a Period of Two Hundred Years* (Philadelphia, Pa.: Lindsay and Blakiston, 1853), microfiche, 458.

16.  Sadie Scott Kellam and V. Hope Kellam, *Old Houses in Princess Anne Virginia* (Portsmouth, Va.: Printcraft, 1931), 202.

17.  Katherine Fontaine Syer, "The Town and City of Virginia Beach," in *The History of Lower Tidewater, Virginia,* vol. 2, ed. Rogers Dey Whichard (New York: Lewis Historical Publishing Company, Inc., 1959), 12.

Chapter *3*

# Historic Personalities and Houses

F rom its founding in 1607 until February 1624/5,[1] an estimated 7,549 people arrived in the Virginia colony. Of these, only one in six (or 1,095) were alive and resident during the 1624/5 muster (a list somewhat like a census).[2] The population was decimated by disease, starvation, returns to England, and Indian attacks. The Massacre of 1622, in which Indians attacked the settlers for 140 miles along the James River, claimed the lives of 350 people.[3]

There was more traveling back and forth between England and the Virginia Colony than we might expect. People sometimes returned to England to stay; however, many times they went to England to conduct business, to marry, or to recruit more settlers for the new land. Such recruiting was very lucrative, as a headright (a grant of land) was awarded to the person who paid the passage for each individual who entered the colony. Entry by 1616 was worth 100 acres per person and for entry thereafter, the award was 50 acres per person.[4]

In June 1624 the Virginia Company charter was dissolved, and the colony became administered by the Crown. A muster, which listed the people and supplies in Virginia, was compiled January 20 through February 7, 1624/5. Persons killed in the 1622 massacre were also listed.[5]

Many settlers listed in the muster are noted as "servants." It is suggested that the term "employee" is much more in keeping with the seventeenth century concept than our twentieth century interpretation of the term "servant."[6] Spelling was not standardized in the early colonial period. Even proper nouns and names of families varied. Differences occurred according to the ear of the listener which yielded variations in both vowel and consonant sounds. The same person or members of the same family might use a variety of spelling of the family name during their lifetimes.

Any research into the families that populated the area later known as Princess Anne County reveals a close and sometimes convoluted relationship among them.  With so few people living in the colony, it is understandable that the families became intertwined.  It was not uncommon for men and women to remarry after the death of a spouse.  These tangled relationships seem easier to understand when we examine a few of the families in the young colony.

# Personalities

*Families which became mainstays of social, political, and economic life in Princess Anne were among the very first arrivals.  The following list (in alphabetical order) gives a flavor of the interrelationships of these early families.*

## GOOKIN

Daniel Gookin, who was born in County Kent, England, arrived from Ireland in 1620.  He came on his own ship, the *Flying Harte*, and brought eighty people, cattle, and provisions with him.  He settled in Newport News at Marie's Mount, which was named for his wife.[7]  One son, Daniel, moved from Virginia to Maryland and then Massachusetts for religious reasons.  His descendants were closely associated with Harvard College.  They married members of the Quincy, Eliot, and Cotton families.[8]

The other son, John Gookin, was born circa 1613 and probably arrived in Virginia around 1630.  In 1636 John acquired 500 acres on the Nansemond River.  In the period from 1638 to 1640, he served as a burgess for Upper Norfolk County and a justice for Lower Norfolk County.  In 1641 he acquired 640 acres in what became Princess Anne County.  In 1640 or 1641 he married Sarah Offley Thorowgood, the widow of his neighbor Adam Thorowgood.[9]  John died November 2, 1643.[10]  John and Sarah had a daughter, Mary, who was born in 1642.  In adulthood she married Captain William Moseley.  After Moseley's death in 1671, she married Lieutenant Colonel Anthony Lawson.  Her descendants connected with the Sayer, Thorowgood, Lawson, Moore, Woodhouse,[11] Moseley, Walke, Bassett, and Calvert families.[12]

## OFFLEY

Robert Offley was a merchant in London who dealt in goods from Turkey. He was also a member of the Virginia Company, 1609 and a stockholder in the company in 1619. Both his father-in-law and his grandfather-in-law had been Lord Mayor of London.[13] He was deeply involved in the Virginia colony but did not visit it. Two of his daughters, however, married and moved to Virginia. His daughter Sarah married Adam Thorowgood in London in 1627 when she was eighteen. She accompanied him when he returned to Virginia.[14] Following his death in 1640,[15] Sarah married their neighbor Captain John Gookin who died in 1643. She married Colonel Francis Yeardley in 1647, and he lived until 1655.[16] During their marriages, each husband lived with Sarah at the manor house willed to her by Adam Thorowgood.[17]

Sarah must have been an interesting person, as there are stories still told about her 300 years after her death. One describes a Lower Norfolk court session held at William Shipp's on August 3, 1640. The wife

> *of a vestryman made insinuations as to sharp business practices on the part of the late Captain Thorowgood, where-upon the widow exclaimed, "Why, Goody Layton, could you never get yours?" (referring to a canceled note which had been paid.) The lady flounced around and cried, "Pish!" To which Mistress Sarah replied, "You must not think to put it off with a 'pish!' for if you have wronged him you must answer for it, for though he is dead I am here in his behalf to right him." The "goody" was required by court order to ask Mistress Sarah's forgiveness on her knees, both in Court and on the following Sunday in the Parish Church at Lynnhaven.*[18]

Sarah Offley Thorowgood Gookin Yeardley died in August 1657 at the age of forty-eight. She requested that she be buried next to her second husband, Captain John Gookin.[19] She also requested that her "'best' diamond necklace" be "sold in England to pay for six diamond rings (probably mourning rings) and two black tombstones as was indicated in a receipt for and agreement to sell the necklace executed by Nicholas Trott, merchant, on February 1, 1657/8."[20] Her armorial tombstone was still visible at Church Point as late as 1819, when its inscription was published in a Richmond newspaper.[21] It read, "Here lieth ye body of Capt. John Gooking & also ye body of Mrs. Sarah Yardley who was wife to Captain Adam Thorowgood first, Capt. John Gooking & Collonel Francis Yardley, who deceased August 1657."[22] There are several transcriptions of this tombstone. They vary only in spelling and abbreviations, while the text remains consistent.

Sarah had lived in London and in Virginia, married three influential men, conducted business in the courts, and was the mother of five children who lived to maturity (four Thorowgood children[23] and one Gookin child).[24]

Robert Offley had another daughter, Anne, who first married a Mr. Workman. Her second marriage was to Robert Hayes, who had a patent of 100 acres on the Lynnhaven River. He had received this patent for the transportation of the two of them in 1637/8. Robert Hayes kept the ferry at Little Creek and served as a burgess and vestryman. In 1643 he patented an additional 750 acres adjoining the land of his deceased brother-in-law, Captain Adam Thorowgood. The land patent was granted for the importation of fifteen people, including the Wortman (Workman) children and his own children, Alex. and Nathaniel Hayes.[25]

## THOROWGOOD/THOROUGHGOOD

*The name we commonly spell* Thoroughgood *was generally spelled* Thorowgood *until the mid-1800s.*

Adam Thorowgood was the seventh son of the vicar of St. Botolph's Church in Grimston, Norfolk, England. He came to Virginia on the *Charles* in 1621 and in the 1624/5 muster was listed as eighteen years old and a "servant" of Mr. Edward Waters of Elizabeth City.[26] Here is one case where the twentieth century interpretation of "servant" seems an unlikely circumstance. Adam Thorowgood was a member of a large family and although his father was a clergyman, two of his brothers were known as Sir Edward and Sir John Thorowgood.[27] Additionally, in 1626, within two years of being listed as a servant, he had purchased 150 acres on the north side of Hampton Roads. He left Virginia sometime after December 1626 and married Sarah Offley in London the following summer. By 1628 he had returned to Virginia with his wife, Sarah, and 105 persons for whom he paid passage, receiving 50 acres per person.[28] He settled on the western bank of the Lynnhaven River, which was previously called the Chesapeake River.

Adam Thorowgood has traditionally been credited with associating the name Lynnhaven with this area.[29] His home in Grimston was only about eight miles from King's Lynn in Norfolk County, England. The name certainly fits the physical description of the area as the term *linn* (or *lynn*) means pool, cascade, or waterfall.[30] The word *haven* means a recess or inlet of the sea, the mouth of a river, a harbor, or a port.[31] The namegiver would have known these terms as they were in common usage at the time.

Adam Thorowgood died in 1640 at the age of thirty-five. His will was probated on April 27 of that year in Quarter Court at James City, rather than in the Lower Norfolk County court. This raises the possibility that he may have died in Jamestown while attending a council session. In view of his position as a council member, probate in the Quarter Court would have been quite natural. Sarah Thorowgood, his wife, was named executrix in his will and inherited, along with a portion of the estate, the Manor House Plantation for life. Their son Adam inherited the rest of his father's houses and lands in Virginia. He would also inherit the Manor House Plantation after Sarah's death. Adam Thorowgood also bequeathed 1,000 pounds of tobacco to the Lynnhaven Parish Church to buy "some necessary and decent ornaments" and directed that he be buried in the churchyard at Church Point beside some of his children.[32]

Sarah and Adam Thorowgood's eldest son, Adam, found himself in the midst of a complicated family relationship. In 1646 he married Frances, the daughter of Argoll Yeardley and granddaughter of the former colonial governor, Sir George Yeardley. This meant that his stepfather, Colonel Francis Yeardley, was also his uncle by marriage. Upon his mother Sarah's death in 1657, he came into his complete inheritance and probably moved his wife, Frances, and their family, Argoll, John, Adam III, Francis, Robert, and Rose into the Manor House Plantation which Sarah had occupied.

When the "Colonel," as he had become known, made his will in 1679, he provided for his wife, Frances, as his father had done for Sarah, by leaving her the Manor House Plantation and 600 acres for life. Upon her death the plantation would go to his eldest son, Argoll. The remainder of his land and houses were to be divided in five equal parts, one for each of the sons according to their choice in order of seniority. Colonel Adam Thorowgood died in 1685/6.[33] Over the years the Thorowgood family connected with, among others, the Yeardley, Church, Lawson, Keeling, Nimmo, Woodhouse, Sayer,[34] Custis, Fowke, and Mason families.[35]

## WOODHOUSE

Captain Henry Woodhouse, also from Norfolk County, England, was a member of the Virginia Company, 1609. He served as governor of Bermuda and was from a highly connected family. He was the son of Sir Henry Woodhouse and his wife, Ann Bacon. Ann was the daughter of the Lord Keeper of the Seal and the sister to the Lord Chancellor of England.[36]

Henry Woodhouse (son of Captain Henry and grandson of Sir Henry) patented a headright in 1637 for 500 acres located near the Lynnhaven Inlet. Henry Woodhouse was an attorney and served as justice, burgess, and vestrymember.[37] In the generations between their arrival in the colonies and the early 1700s, the Woodhouse family became connected to the Collins, Bennett, Attwood, Keeling, Moore, and Malbone families.[38]

## YEARDLEY

The Yeardley family was also headed by a shareholder of the Virginia Company, 1609. George Yeardley first arrived in Virginia in 1610 following an ill-fated voyage. He had been aboard the *Seaventure* which wrecked in Bermuda as the result of a hurricane. After his belated arrival in Virginia, he became co-commander of Forts Henry and Charles. About 1613 he married Temperence Flowerdew, previously of Norfolk County, England. She had arrived in the colony in 1609. George Yeardley was deputy governor of the colony by 1616. He and Temperance returned to England where they remained until 1618, the year George Yeardley was knighted. He was sent to Virginia as governor and arrived in 1619.[39] During his administration the first representative legislature was convened in the New World.[40] Following his term as governor, the Yeardleys chose to remain in Virginia. In 1626 George was reappointed governor, a position he held until his death in November 1627.

In 1647 one of their sons, Francis, married Sarah Offley, who was the widow of Adam Thorowgood and of John Gookin. Francis's career in politics appears to have been somewhat checkered. He was appointed to the Maryland Council in 1652 but only served a few months. In 1653/4 he had some legal problems, again in Maryland. He was found guilty of illegally seizing a ship and fined 3,000 pounds of tobacco. In the same year, he was charged with "contemptuous carriage and demeanor" toward the Maryland government. Meanwhile, in 1653, he served as a burgess for Lower Norfolk County. He was also a justice. He had died by 1656, leaving no children.[41]

# *Houses*

*Several of the houses which were built in the early years of Princess Anne County are currently open to the public. Families which ranged from ordinary gentry to families of wealth lived in these homes.*

## FRANCIS LAND HOUSE

3131 Virginia Beach Boulevard
Owner: City of Virginia Beach

The Francis Land House is a fine example of the Georgian architectural style that the landed gentry preferred during the second half of the eighteenth century. The house was once thought to have been built in 1732, as there is a brick in the cellar which has those numbers on it. That date is now considered unrealistic. Discussions with Colonial Williamsburg staff revealed that the construction style of the flooring was not in general use prior to the American Revolution. Also, the interior brickwork in the cellar (three rows of stretchers and one row of headers)[42] was not in common use until about 1810.[43] Additionally, in 1992, a dendrochronology analysis, a scientific dating process in which the wood used in construction is dated to its last growing year, was done at the Francis Land House. It indicates that the last year of tree growth was 1804.[44] These items taken together yield a construction date in the late eighteenth/early nineteenth century time frame.[45]

The house is built of handmade brick (probably made nearby) laid in Flemish bond.[46] The mortar has a significant content of ground oyster shells. The front door opens into a central passage which, along with the dining room on the right, retains much of its original pine woodwork.[47] The parlor on the left side of the passage is the largest room in the house. A chamber behind the dining room was probably used for sleeping.[48]

The gambrel roof is a distinctive feature and helps to date the house closer to the end of the eighteenth century. The roof was raised approximately twenty inches in 1912, creating a full second story. A brick well remnant has been uncovered behind the house. Twentieth century additions and changes have made the cellar an accessible space.[49]

Six generations of Francis Lands lived on the property from the 1630s until 1819, running a successful plantation with the use of slave labor. In 1819 Francis Moseley Land (the sixth Francis) died and his personal property was auctioned. However, his daughters, Mary and Ann, inherited his real property. By 1853 neither the house nor the property was owned by Land descendants.[50]

The house was associated with farming operations until the 1950s, when Colin and Mary Studds purchased the building and opened a fashionable dress shop called "Rose Hall."[51] The Francis Land House was purchased by the City of Virginia Beach in 1975[52] and has been open to the public since 1986.

## LYNNHAVEN HOUSE

4401 Wishart Road
Owner: Association for the Preservation of Virginia Antiquities

This brick house, on a finger of the Lynnhaven River, was known for many years as the Wishart House or the Boush House. For clarity and

**Lynnhaven House**, circa 1725

Courtesy of the Virginia Beach Public Library

due to its proximity to Lynnhaven Bay, it is now called the Lynnhaven House. For many years it was assumed that the Lynnhaven House was built in the mid-to-late 1600s.[53] The scientific dating process, dendrochronology, however, places the house at a much later date. During the process, samples of wood from the floor joists were analyzed.[54] The results indicated that the timbers were cut in the winter of 1724/5.[55] This date suggests that the house was built by Francis Thelaball, who owned the property at that time.

The inventory of Thelaball's estate, taken after his death in 1727, lists furnishings that would have been owned by a man of beyond modest, but not wealthy, means. There was an absence of prints for the walls, silver, or a list of books. However, the value of the fabric on the beds; enumeration of table linens; a parcel of glass, knives and forks; new and old pewter; and a case of bottles show a level of refinement in the lifestyle enjoyed by the Thelaball family. The estate also listed three boats, cattle, horses, and sheep.[56]

The Lynnhaven House is constructed of brick in the English bond pattern and has two massive gable-end chimneys.[57] It is a story-and-a-half structure with two rooms down and two rooms above. The main door opens directly into the south room (the hall), a multi-purpose room. The north room on the first floor is the kitchen, which contains a very large cooking fireplace. The Lynnhaven House is an excellent example of early eighteenth century Tidewater Virginia vernacular architecture.[58] The William W. Oliver, Sr. family presented it as a gift to the Association for the Preservation of Virginia Antiquities in 1971 on the condition that it be restored as a historic monument.[59]

## THOROUGHGOOD HOUSE

1136 Parish Road
Owner: Chrysler Museum

Early researchers had assumed that the Thoroughgood House was Captain Adam Thorowgood's Manor Plantation. However, the manor house is now believed to have been situated in the vicinity of Baylake Pines.[60] Current research on the Thoroughgood House suggests a date of circa 1680.[61] The house was remodeled in the early part of the eighteenth century. The interior floor plan was altered slightly and oak panels and wainscoting were installed. The west wall features Flemish bond brickwork and differs from the two gables and the east wall, which are of English bond. In 1957 the house was acquired by the Adam Thoroughgood House Foundation, headed by Henry Clay Hofheimer II. It was restored under the direction of Finlay F. Ferguson, Jr., an architect formerly associated with Colonial Williamsburg.[62]

During the restoration it was discovered that the seventeenth century leaded mullion casement windows had been replaced by Georgian sash windows. The lack of a central hall was another seventeenth century feature of the house. The entrance went directly into the larger of two downstairs rooms. The addition of a partition parallel to the original inner wall remodeled the downstairs into two rooms, with a central hall in between.[63]

According to Floyd Painter, a local archaeologist who conducted excavations at the Thoroughgood House, the site had once been that of a Chesapeake Indian village. The numerous Indian artifacts indicate that it may possibly have been the principal Chesapeake town.[64]

**Adam Thoroughgood House**, circa 1680

Courtesy of the Virginia Beach Public Library

## UPPER WOLFSNARE
2040 Potters Road
Owner: Princess Anne County/Virginia Beach Historical Society

This eighteenth century two-story English bond house, with a basement and an attic, stands on land acquired by Thomas Walke III in the 1700s. He probably started building "the brick house" around 1759.[65] Upper Wolfsnare has been essentially restored to its original form. Previously known as the Brick House Farm,[66] or the old Walke Place, it is now known as Upper Wolfsnare. The word "Upper" distinguishes it from Wolfsnare Plantation which is nearby.

The house was the manor for a plantation of 7,000 acres, much livestock, fifty-five slaves, and a mill. Although plain, it was built with the finest materials. The house has corner fireplaces which are shared between two rooms. Especially noteworthy is its fine woodwork, particularly in the wide central hall.[67]

Thomas Walke IV inherited the house from his father and was residing there in 1788 when he served as one of Princess Anne County's two elected delegates to the Virginia convention at which the state ratified the United States Constitution.[68] Thomas Walke IV died childless and the house changed hands many times. Various members of the Boush, Cornick, Ferebee, Fentress, Worrell, and Malbon families (among others) owned the house.

In 1964 the Commonwealth of Virginia purchased the house to insure a right-of-way for the Norfolk-Virginia Beach Expressway. The state had planned to demolish Upper Wolfsnare and use the land for fill during the road project. An agreement was reached between the highway department and the Princess Anne Historical Society, which enabled a land trade to save the house. Mr. and Mrs. James Sadler owned adjacent land that was used as road fill, thus saving Upper Wolfsnare. The property was deeded to the Princess Anne Historical Society.[69]

An archaeological dig took place on the site in 1979. Because the area had been lived on and farmed for hundreds of years, there were few remaining early artifacts. However, portions of Chinese export porcelain, fine pearlwares, case bottles, and a wine bottle seal were found. These all indicate that a family of some substance lived in the house between 1760 and the early 1800s.[70]

# Notes for Chapter 3

1.  Dates listed with a slash indicate both the Julian and the Gregorian years. The dates concerned are between January 1 and March 25 (the Julian New Year) until the year 1752 when the calendars were consolidated. For instance, 20 February 1652/3 means that the date was 1652 in the Julian calendar and 1653 in the Gregorian calendar.
2.  Virginius Dabney, *Virginia, the New Dominion* (Charlottesville, Va.: University Press of Virginia, 1982), 36.
3.  Ibid., 35.
4.  Virginia M. Meyer and John Frederick Dorman, eds., *Adventurers of Purse and Person: Virginia 1607-1624/5*, 3rd ed., (Richmond, Va.: Dietz Press, Inc., 1987), xxvi.
5.  Ibid., 3.
6.  Ibid., xxviii.
7.  Ibid., 311-312.
8.  Ibid., 316-318.
9.  Ibid., 314.
10. "Gookin Family," in *Genealogies of Virginia Families from the Virginia Magazine of History and Biography.* vol. 5, Randolph-Zouch (Baltimore, Md.: Genealogical Publishing Co., Inc., 1981), 690.
11. Meyer and Dorman, eds., 318-319.
12. "Gookin Family," 691.
13. Meyer and Dorman, eds., 459.
14. Ibid., 460.
15. Ibid., 608.
16. Ibid., 727.
17. Rogers Dey Whichard, *The History of Lower Tidewater Virginia*, vol.1 (New York: Lewis Historical Publishing Company, Inc., 1959), 263.
18. Ibid., 266.
19. George Carrington Mason, *Colonial Churches of Tidewater Virginia* (Richmond, Va.: Whittet and Shepperson, 1945), 132.
20. Whichard, vol.1, 275.
21. Mason, 132.
22. Whichard, vol.1, 253.
23. Meyer and Dorman, eds., 609.
24. Ibid., 315.
25. Ibid., 459-460.
26. Ibid., 608.
27. "Thoroughgood Family," in *Genealogies of Virginia Families from the Virginia Magazine of History and Biography*, vol. 5, Randolph-Zouch (Baltimore, Md.: Genealogical Publishing Co., Inc., 1981), 482.
28. Meyer and Dorman, eds., 608-609.
29. Mason, 128.
30. *Oxford English Dictionary*, 2nd ed., s.v. "linn."
31. Ibid., s.v. "haven."
32. Whichard, vol.1, 262-263.
33. Ibid., 264.
34. "Thoroughgood Family," 482.
35. Meyer and Dorman, eds., 699.
36. Ibid., 699
37. Ibid., 700.
38. Ibid., 699-703.
39. Ibid., 724-725.
40. "George Yeardley," in *Genealogies of Virginia Families from the Virginia Magazine of History and Biography*, vol. 5, Randolph-Zouch (Baltimore, Md.: Genealogical Publishing Co., Inc., 1981), 918.
41. Meyer and Dorman, eds., 727.
42. A stretcher is the long side of a brick and a header is the short end of a brick. Brickwork patterns and styles have changed over time and can be useful in dating a structure.
43. Mark Reed, letter to the author, 24 April 1996.

44. Herman J. Heikkenen, *The Last Year of Tree Growth for Selected Timbers within the Francis Land House as Derived by Key-Year Dendrochronology* (Blacksburg, Va.: Dendrochronology, Inc., 1992.)

45. Mark Reed, 24 April 1996.

46. Flemish bond is a pattern in which brick was laid. Stretchers (the long side of the brick) were laid in an alternating pattern with headers (the short end of the brick) in the same horizontal row. Vertically, the stretchers were placed over the headers in the lower row. This pattern is said to have become popular after the 1666 Great Fire of London. English bond refers to a pattern of brickwork where stretchers and headers make up individual rows which are laid in an alternating pattern vertically, stretchers upon headers.

47. City of Virginia Beach,Va. The Office of Research and Strategic Analysis. *City of Virginia Beach Inventory of Historic Buildings and Sites* (Virginia Beach, Va.: City of Virginia Beach, 1990), March 1990, 4-13.

48. Mark Reed, letter to the author, 13 April 1996.

49. Ibid.

50. Mark Reed, 24 April 1996.

51. Mark Reed, 13 April 1996.

52. Bert Rohrer, "Beach Council Okays Purchase of Rose Hall," *Virginian-Pilot*, 17 June 1975, section A, 3.

53. Mary Reid Barrow, "No Historical Lies," *Virginia Beach Beacon*, 1 July 1983, 22.

54. Mary Reid Barrow, "Lynnhaven House Has a Burgeoning Past," *Virginia Beach Beacon*, 16 February 1986, 6.

55. Herman John Heikkenen, *Final Report: The Year of Construction of the Lynnhaven House as Derived by Key-year Dendrochronology Technique* (Blacksburg,Va.: The American Institute of Dendrochronology, 1982)

56. *Princess Anne County Will Book*, 1724-1735, 129.

57. Betty Pettinger, "17th Century House Called One of the Best Preserved in the U.S.," *Richmond* (Va.) *Times Dispatch*, 4 September 1974, section A, 8.

58. Marilyn S. Melchor, letter to the author, April 1996.

59. City of Virginia Beach,Va. The Office of Research and Strategic Analysis, March 1990, 4-13

60. Florence Kimberly Turner, *Gateway to the New World: A History of Princess Anne County, Virginia, 1609-1824* (Easley, S.C.: Southern Historical Press, 1985), 35.

61. "Chrysler Museum, Historic Houses," (typescript, n.d., acquired January 1996), unpaged.

62. Joanne Young, "Brick House Here Believed Oldest in America to be Dedicated Monday; Restoration Complete," *Virginian-Pilot*, 27 April 1957, 7.

63. George H Tucker, "17th Century Shrine Scene of Ceremony," *Virginian-Pilot*, 30 April 1957, 10.

64. Floyd Painter, "Artifacts from the Thoroughgood Site," *The Chesopiean*, 3, December 1965, 130.

65. Stephen S. Mansfield, *Princess Anne County and Virginia Beach: A Pictorial History* (Virginia Beach, Va.: The Donning Company/Publishers, 1989), 35.

66. Sadie Scott Kellam and V. Hope Kellam, *Old Houses in Princess Anne Virginia* (Portsmouth,Va.: Printcraft, 1931), 195.

67. City of Virginia Beach,Va. The Office of Research and Stategic Analysis, March 1990, 4-13.

68. Mansfield, 214.

69. Louisa Venable Kyle, "Upper Wolf Snare Plantation" (typescript, 1971).

70. Andrew C. Edwards and Norman F. Barka, *The Archaeology of Upper Wolfsnare, Virginia Beach, Virginia* (Williamsburg, Va.: The College of Willam and Mary, 1979), vi-vii.

# Chapter 4

# Witches and Witchcraft

W itchcraft is an ancient system of belief which has come into vogue periodically throughout the ages. While colonial history tends to focus on the witch trials in Salem, Massachusetts, numerous trials were also held in Princess Anne County. A 1655 Lower Norfolk County court order stated that anyone making an accusation of witchcraft was liable for a fine, and a possible censure by the court, if he was unable to prove his charge under oath and with witnesses.[1] In December 1659, the court enforced its ruling by fining Thomas Godby 300 pounds of tobacco, along with court costs of twenty pounds of tobacco, because his wife, Ann, made an unsubstantiated accusation of witchcraft against Mrs. Nicholas Robinson.[2]

Nearly twenty years passed before the county court recorded John Samon's accusation against Alice Cartwrite concerning the death of his child, whom Alice was said to have bewitched. An all-female jury searched Alice's body for marks indicative of the occult. Finding none, they acquitted her.[3]

On July 8, 1698, John and Anne Byrd were the plaintiffs in two separate defamation suits. Charles Kinsey had accused Anne of being a witch and testified that she had ridden him from his house. That same day the Byrds again appeared in court, suing John Pitt for accusing them of being in league with the devil. Pitt claimed that the Byrds had ridden him along the seashore to his home. The Byrds lost both suits.[4] Although these suits are hardly what one associates with witchcraft trials, they were the forerunners of the trials of Grace Sherwood, popularly known as the "Witch of Pungo."

Beginning in February 1697, there were a series of suits for slander initiated by Grace and James Sherwood against Richard Capps, John and Jane Gisburne, and Anthony and Elizabeth Barnes. These people had previously accused the Sherwoods of witchcraft. The suit against

Capps was amicably settled and dismissed.  However, the Gisburnes insisted that Grace had bewitched their cotton.  The Barneses contended that Grace had come to Elizabeth in the night, ridden her, and "gone out of the Key hole or crack of the door like a black Catt."[5]  These trials lasted four days with the same all-male jury impaneled for both suits.  The fact that both verdicts were against the Sherwoods seems to have been a sign of things to come.[6]

In 1701 James Sherwood died and Grace became the administratrix of his small estate.  Four years later court records show that Grace sued Luke Hill and his wife for trespassing, assault, and battery.  Grace was awarded only twenty shillings and court costs.  Mark Powell, the jury foreman, neglected to sign the verdict, so the judgment had to be carried over until the next term.[7]  Powell had previously been a juror in the 1698 suits of the Sherwoods against the Gisburnes and the Barneses.[8]

On February 6, 1705, the Hills made a formal complaint against Grace on suspicion of witchcraft.  The following March the court summoned a jury of women to search Grace's person for any telltale marks indicative of a witch.  It is not surprising that their search was successful, since the

Charles Sibley. **Witch Ducking in 1706, Grace Sherwood**

Courtesy of the Old Coast Guard Station and Charles Sibley

forewoman of the jury was the same Elizabeth Barnes who had been the defendant in previous litigation involving the Sherwoods.[9]

Though the jury claimed to have found marks on Grace, the court was apprehensive about passing judgment. Luke Hill appealed to the

---

*July 10th 1706*

*Whearas Grace Sherwood being Suspected of witchcraft have a long time waited for a ffit uppertunity ffor a ffurther Examinacon and by her Consent & approbacon of ye Court it is ordr yt ye Sherr take all Such Convenient assistance of boate & men as Shall be by him thought ffit to meet at Jon Harpers plantacon in ordr to take ye Sd Grace forth with & but her into above mans Debth and try her how She Swims Therein alwayes having Care of her life to prserve her from Drowning & as Soon as She Comes Out yt he request as many Ansient & knowing women as possible he Cann to Serch her Carefully ffor all teats spotts & marks about her body not usuall in Others & yt as they ffind ye Same to make report on Oath To ye truth thereof to ye Court & further it is ordr yt Som women be requested to Shift & Serch her before She goe into ye water yt She Carry nothing about her to cause any ffurther Suspicion.*

**Transcribed Court Order**

*The Lower Norfolk County Virginia Antiquary*, NY: Peter Smith, 1951, vol. 3, p. 36

---

attorney general, Stephen Thompson, in Williamsburg. This higher court refused to hear the case because it was too general and did not charge Grace with a particular act. The case was returned to the jurisdiction of the county. More hearings were held during the next several months, and finally in July 1706, Grace consented to a trial by ducking. Scheduled for July 5, the ducking was postponed until Wednesday, July 10 due to inclement weather.[10]

On that day Grace was brought to John Harper's plantation on the Lynnhaven River. She was tied in the manner customary for ducking, her right thumb to her left toe and her left thumb to her right toe, and cast into the river. It was believed that a witch would not sink, and Grace managed to stay afloat. The crowd of spectators and the women designated to search her after the ordeal judged her to be a witch. The sheriff took her into custody for future trial. She was imprisoned in the county jail but eventually released.  There is no evidence that any further action was taken against her.[11]

Grace Sherwood, the alleged "Witch of Pungo," is the subject of much local folklore.  At her ducking she is said to have told the spectators, "not one of ye will see me ducked.  But I'll see all of ye ducked."[12] The day was beautifully clear, but just as she was taken out of the water a terrible storm came up.  The fury of the thunder, lightning, and rain sent the crowd into a panic, while Grace stood by calmly watching.[13]

It is said that one night Grace needed some rosemary.  Discovering that a ship was anchored off Lynnhaven Town, she sailed to it in an eggshell and bewitched the cabin boy.  She then summoned a strong wind, sailed the ship to England, and returned the same night with a sprig of rosemary.  Legend has it that the rosemary bushes in Princess Anne County came from the sprig that Grace brought back from England.  It is also told that once, while she was waiting to be hanged, Grace asked a boy to bring her two unwashed pewter plates.  When he handed the plates to her, she put one under each arm and promptly flew off across Currituck Sound, escaping her execution.[14]

One of the strangest events concerning Grace is said to have taken place at her death in 1740.[15]  As she lay ill during a fierce storm, Grace asked her sons to move her from her bed and place her feet into the warm ashes of the fireplace.  During the night a tremendous gust of wind came down the chimney, scattering embers everywhere.  When Grace's sons looked in on her, they discovered that she had disappeared.  All that remained of their mother was the imprint of a cloven hoof in the ashes.[16]

## Notes for Chapter 4

1.  Benjamin Dey White, "Gleanings in the History of Princess Anne County," in *An Economic and Social Survey of Princess Anne County* (Charlottesville, Va.: Michie Company, 1924), 13.

2.  Edward W. James, *The Lower Norfolk County Virginia Antiquary,* vol. IV, (New York: Peter Smith, 1951), 36.

3.  Ibid., vol. I, 56-57.

4.  Ibid., vol. I, 20-21.

5.  Ibid., vol. II, 93.

6.  Ibid., vol. II, 92-93.

7.  Ibid., vol. II, 139-140.

8.  Ibid., vol. II, 93.

9.  Ibid., vol. II, 140-141.

10.  Ibid., vol. III, 35-36.

11.  George Holbert Tucker, "Grace Sherwood of History and Legend: Princess Ann's Double Witch," *Norfolk Virginian-Pilot*, 13 November 1949, Part 5, 1.

12.  W. H. T. Squires, *The Days of Yester-Year in Colony and Commonwealth* (Portsmouth, Va.: Printcraft Press, Inc., 1928), 74.

13.  Ibid.

14.  Agnes White Thomas, "Princess Anne's Own: Meet Grace Sherwood - A Genuine Witch," *Virginian-Pilot and the Portsmouth Star*, 28 April 1957, section E, 1.

15.  George H. Tucker, "Tidewater Landfalls: Devil in Princess Anne," *Virginian-Pilot*, 23 July 1959, 25.

16.  Tucker, "Grace Sherwood of History and Legend," 11.

*Chapter* 5

# *Pirates*

From the earliest days of the English settlements in the New World, piracy flourished in the coastal waters of North America.[1] When Sir Francis Wyatt arrived in Virginia to be governor in 1621, he came with numerous instructions from the Crown on its governance. Of primary importance was his instruction to punish piracies and to build fortresses for the defense of the colony.[2]

According to historian Hugh E. Rankin, the golden age of piracy began about 1630 in Tortuga with the formation of the "Confederacy of the Brethren of the Coast," a pirate "republic."[3] By the late 1720s, however, the guardships of the British Royal Navy had put an end to piracy's golden era.

During this golden age of piracy, there was extensive trade between the newly formed colonies in the Americas and their home countries in Europe. Due to the great distances involved and the unfamiliarity with unknown waters, policing the waters of the colonies was very difficult, leaving many merchant ships vulnerable to attack by pirates and other hostile vessels.[4]

During the seventeenth century, Spain, England, Holland, and France, warred with one another frequently. The warring nations would "license" privateers to attack and loot an enemy's ships. When peace was declared, many privateers, unwilling to abandon lucrative careers, turned to piracy.[5]

The rich commerce of Virginia made the cargo-laden vessels of the Chesapeake Bay tempting targets for pirates. Forts had been established in the colony for protection, but by 1691 most of Virginia's forts were in very poor condition. Land fortifications were not a sufficient safeguard from pirates and privateers, so Virginia turned to guardships from England for protection.[6] Because of the threat of pirate attack, merchant ships were ordered to assemble at a given point in the Chesapeake Bay (often Point Comfort or Lynnhaven Bay) and sail in convoy under the protection of a guardship.[7]

In July of 1699, the waters of Lynnhaven Bay were terrorized by a pirate ship, the *Alexander* (originally named *Providence Frigate* and also known as *Providence Galley*),[8] commanded by John James.  Having learned of the vulnerability of Virginia's naval defenses from record books taken from a captured ship, James saw his opportunity to plunder Virginia's waters with impunity.  The Virginia guardship *Essex Prize*, commanded by Captain John Aldred, engaged the pirate ship in battle, but being outgunned and undermanned, the guardship withdrew.  The *Alexander* went on to loot two merchant ships, *Maryland Merchant* and *Roanoke Merchant*, and then left the area unhindered.[9]

Virginia's government was greatly alarmed by these attacks and was also concerned about possible pirate landings.  The need for a larger, more powerful guardship was apparent, and Governor Sir Francis Nicholson appealed to the king for help.[10]  The governor also ordered the militias in the counties of Norfolk, Princess Anne, Accomack, Northampton, and Elizabeth City to post lookouts to patrol the shores, looking for strange or suspicious sails.  One such lookout patrolled the beach between Cape Henry and Lynnhaven River.[11]

In April 1700 the French pirate ship *La Paix*, commanded by Frenchman Louis Guittar, practically brought shipping in Virginia to a halt.  After taking a number of vessels near the capes, Guittar sailed into Lynnhaven Bay and began plundering vessels anchored there.[12]  Edward Whittaker was the master of the *Indian King*, a ship that Guittar had plundered outside the capes.  Guittar questioned Whittaker about the threat of guardships in Virginia's waters.  Whittaker told him about the *Essex Prize*, a sixth-rater, which he believed had returned to England.[13] (British warships were rated according to the number of guns they carried.  There were six rates, with first-rate being the most powerful, sixth-rate being the least.  First-rate ships carried 100 guns or more, sixth-raters carried up to 32.[14]  The *Essex Prize* had only 16 guns.)[15]  Feeling safe from the threat of colonial guardships, *La Paix* went on to plunder nine ships whose combined cargo was valued at £20,000.[16]

Unbeknownst to Guittar, the British man-of-war *Shoreham*, commanded by Captain William Passenger, had arrived to replace the *Essex Prize*.  Alerted to the presence of the pirate ship by a small vessel on its way down the Chesapeake Bay, Governor Nicholson ordered the *Shoreham* to set sail to engage *La Paix*.  Governor Nicholson and Captain Aldred were also aboard the *Shoreham*.[17]  After ten hours of fierce fighting, the pirate ship ran aground at Lynnhaven and was forced to strike her colors and surrender.[18] Captain Guittar and sixty-four of his pirate crew were sent to England in chains where they were tried and convicted.  On November 23, 1700, Guittar and twenty-three of his companions were hanged.  Soon afterwards, forty others met the same fate.[19]

Three members of the pirate crew, however, were not on board *La Paix* when she surrendered and so were not included in the Articles of Capitulation. John Houghling, the pilot, had jumped overboard and was apprehended near Lynnhaven after swimming ashore. Cornelius Franc and Francois Delaunee were aboard the previously captured merchant vessels when *La Paix* surrendered. All three were tried in a special Court of Admiralty in Elizabeth City. They were convicted and it was ordered that they be turned over to the custody of Sheriff Major John Thorowgood of Princess Anne County for execution. They escaped to Accomack but were recaptured and returned to Princess Anne County, where they were hanged in chains.[20]

Unfortunately, the capture of *La Paix*'s crew did not herald the end of piracy in Virginia. During the early part of the eighteenth century, Virginia and North Carolina were victimized by the notorious pirate Blackbeard. Although his identity is obscure, it is generally accepted that Blackbeard was Edward Teach, a seaman from Bristol, England.

During the reign of Queen Anne, Blackbeard was a privateer, attacking and looting only the enemies of the queen. When peace came to England in 1713, he turned to piracy. He captured a French merchant ship, outfitted her with forty cannons, renamed her *Queen Anne's Revenge*, and preyed on colonial commerce.[21]

Blackbeard was granted the king's "pardon" from North Carolina's governor, Charles Eden, who was intimidated by Blackbeard and lacked the strength to confront his ruthless acts of piracy.[22] Blackbeard took up residence in Bath, North Carolina, becoming a local celebrity. He was able to plunder with immunity and made the shallow sounds of North Carolina's Outer Banks his base of operations. From here, the trade-rich waters of Virginia to the north were an easy mark, as were the waters of Charleston to the south.[23]

Locally, legends of Blackbeard and his buried treasure abound. There is an island in Lake Joyce that is now known as Blackbeard's Island. It is an old breastwork, or fort, and was at one time called Pirate's Fort. Tradition has it that this island was created by pirates. According to W. H. T. Squires in *The Days of Yester-Year in Colony and Commonwealth*, "the firm land originally thrust a point into the calm and clear waters of the bay, in the shape of the letter V. The pirates dug a canal across the little cape which made it an islet, at no mean labor for the canal is approximately twenty-five feet wide."[24] The excavated soil was thrown up on the island side creating an artificial hill. It was believed that pirate sentinels watched vessels entering Virginia's capes from this location. Even after two-and-a-half centuries of erosion, this hill remains a prominent elevation, rising about twenty feet above the canal.

Death of Black Beard.

### *Death of Blackbeard*

Blackbeard meets his demise on board the *Jane*, the ship of British Navy
Lieutenant Robert Maynard.

Courtesy of the Mariners' Museum, Newport News, Virginia

Historians believe that Lake Joyce was once part of a continuous waterway from Little Creek to Lynnhaven.[25] Years ago there was an inlet to the bay through these waters. The present inlet, two miles further east, was dug to shorten the route for small boats to the Chesapeake Bay. Over time the egress from Lake Joyce was blocked by shifting sands so it no longer provides access to Lynnhaven Bay.

At one time, it was possible to stand at the summit of Pirate's Fort and see Cape Henry four miles to the east. Blackbeard's Hill, one of the highest dunes of Cape Henry (fifty feet above sea level), could also be seen. According to Squires, "A sentinel on Blackbeard's Hill could easily detect a merchantman miles away, signal the crew at Pirate's Fort, and Blackbeard would be ready, armed and waiting long before his unsuspecting victim had turned into the channel at Cape Henry."[26]

Today, Blackbeard's Island is privately owned. The view from the island to the east is blocked by dense foliage and by the construction of houses in the area. The exact location of what was called Blackbeard's Hill is now unknown. However, in First Landing/Seashore State Park on the south side of Shore Drive, there exists an ancient sand dune which rises about eighty feet above sea level. The sand dunes are forested, but in winter, when the leaves are gone, one can still see the waters of Virginia's capes and all the ships entering and leaving there.[27]

Blackbeard was a ruthless and cruel man. He once shot one of his own crewmen in the knee, crippling him for life, as a lesson to his crew to remember who he was.[28] He not only threatened merchant ships but also victimized citizens on shore, robbing, plundering, and looting at will. With the immunity under which Blackbeard and other pirates acted in North Carolina, there was a real fear that Ocracoke Island would be turned into a pirate enclave.[29]

The treachery of Blackbeard and his pirate band was so devastating that the North Carolina settlers along Albemarle and Pamlico Sounds clandestinely appealed to Virginia's governor, Alexander Spotswood, for help. The governor, who arrived in Virginia in 1710, was committed to the eradication of piracy in Virginia's waters and was tireless in his pursuit of justice for convicted pirates.[30] He was sympathetic to the appeals made to him from North Carolina for help. Fearing that Virginia's waters would also suffer a similar fate, he resolved to put an end to Blackbeard.[31]

Governor Spotswood's actions against Blackbeard were carried out in great secrecy. There were two reasons for this. First, Spotswood didn't want Blackbeard to be forewarned and escape. Second, sending armed forces into Governor Eden's jurisdiction was an affront to Eden's authority. At his own expense, Spotswood hired two sloops to track Blackbeard down. He also convinced the government of Virginia to offer a £100 reward for Edward Teach, dead or alive.[32]

Lieutenant Robert Maynard set sail from Kecoughtan (now Hampton) on November 17, 1718.  On the morning of November 21, Maynard discovered Blackbeard's two pirate sloops lying at anchor in a sheltered cove in Ocracoke Inlet.  The next day a terrible battle took place.  Coming alongside Maynard's vessel, the *Jane*, Blackbeard and several of his crew boarded the ship and the fighting was hand-to-hand.  Maynard and Blackbeard engaged in a life and death struggle.  When the fighting ended, the decks were littered with the dead and dying.

Blackbeard was killed that day, sustaining no less than twenty-five cut wounds and five pistol shots.[33]  "Hardly had the smoke from the battle cleared, and the moans of the wounded and dying still heavy in the air, than those who remained jubilantly severed Blackbeard's head from his body and hung it from the bowsprit of *Jane*."[34]  In Lloyd Haynes Williams's account he says, "According to tradition, the head dangled for many years from a pole at the mouth of the Hampton River near Kiquotan as a warning to mariners and this place is known even today as Blackbeard's Point."[35]

Fifteen surviving members of Blackbeard's crew were taken to Williamsburg where they were tried by a Court of Admiralty for piracy.  Thirteen were convicted and hanged.[36]

Though piracy in Virginia's waters did not end with Blackbeard's death, piracy was in a rapid decline.  By the late 1720s, the golden age of piracy was over.

## *Notes for Chapter 5*

1. Hugh F. Rankin, *The Golden Age of Piracy* (Williamsburg, Va.: Colonial Williamsburg, 1969), 1.
2. Donald G. Shomette, *Pirates on the Chesapeake* (Centreville, Md.: Tidewater Publishers, 1985), 7.
3. Rankin, 8-9.
4. Lloyd Haynes Williams, *Pirates of Colonial Virginia* (Richmond, Va.: Dietz Press, 1937), 21-22.
5. Nancy Roberts, *Blackbeard and Other Pirates of the Atlantic Coast* (Winston-Salem, N.C.: John F. Blair, Publisher, 1993), xii.
6. Williams, 4-5.
7. Ibid., 7.
8. Shomette, 104.
9. Ibid., 104-110.
10. Ibid., 111.
11. Williams, 51.
12. Ibid., 53.
13. Ibid., 57.
14. Peter Kemp, ed., *The Oxford Companion to Ships and the Sea* (New York: Oxford University Press, 1976), 692.
15. Shomette, 105.
16. Williams, 53.
17. Ibid., 58-59.
18. Robert Beverley, *The History and Present State of Virginia* (Chapel Hill, N.C.: University of North Carolina Press, 1947), 110.
19. Shomette, 150-151.

20. Ibid., 149.
21. W. H. T. Squires, *The Days of Yester-Year In Colony and Commonwealth: A Sketch Book of Virginia* (Portsmouth, Va.: Printcraft Press, Inc., 1928), 50.
22. Shomette, 198-199.
23. Squires, 51.
24. Ibid., 52.
25. Katherine Fontaine Syer, "The County of Princess Anne, 1691-1957," in *The History of Lower Tidewater, Virginia*, vol. 2, ed. Rogers Dey Whichard (New York: Lewis Historical Publishing Company, Inc., 1959), 54.
26. Squires, 54.
27. Philip J. Roehrs, Coastal Engineer, City of Virginia Beach Public Works, Office of Beach Management, telephone interview by author, Virginia Beach, Va., 4 January 1996.
28. Shomette, 203.
29. Ibid., 205.
30. Ibid., 204-216.
31. Ibid., 208.
32. Ibid., 210.
33. Ibid., 214.
34. Ibid., 215.
35. Williams, 113.
36. Shomette, 216.

# Chapter 6

# Cape Henry, Seashore State Park, and the Lighthouses

Cape Henry, the site of the first lighthouse erected by the United States government,[1] has contributed significantly to the history of Virginia Beach. At one time the cape was a sand island, stretching from Stratton's Creek to the Lynnhaven River. Eventually this island became part of the mainland, making up the entire northeast corner of what is now Virginia Beach.

Early sources refer to Cape Henry as "the Desert," a term which is actually misleading. The cape was not made up of desert terrain but was simply an uninhabited stretch of primeval forest. Early sailors often anchored at "the Desert" to replenish their drinking water from the dark cypress pools found there. Cypress water tended to remain fresh for a long period of time, making it especially useful for sea voyages. English settlers, who landed at this spot in 1607, found fresh water springs, many varieties of trees, and dunes 100 feet tall.

Prior to 1770, fishermen often camped on "the Desert." Several gentlemen, including Adam Keeling who owned property to the west of the cape area, applied for patents on this stretch of land. In 1770 the fishermen protested to the governor and Council of State, claiming that such patents would be injurious to their livelihood. The petitioners were apparently successful in their request "that the Land remain a Common for Benefit of the Inhabitants of the Colony in General for Fisheries and other public uses."[2]

The Commonwealth owned "the Desert" until after the American Civil War. During the Reconstruction period, it was sold to lumber companies for the price of one dollar per acre. Due to the remoteness of the area, the lack of adequate transportation, and an extreme mosquito problem, lumbering operations were unsuccessful. In 1902, soon after the seaside resort community of Virginia Beach began to develop, the Chesapeake Transit Company built a railroad to the beach by way

of Cape Henry.  Norfolk businessmen formed the Cape Henry Syndicate
to buy and develop "the Desert."

The Commonwealth purchased the land from the syndicate and by
1936 had created Virginia Seashore State Park.  Benjamin B. Burroughs
was responsible for the formation of the Virginia Seashore State Park
Association, and he became its first president.  Six hundred workers
from the Civilian Conservation Corps spent months building roads,
trails, and cabins in order to make the natural beauty of the park
accessible to visitors.

Seashore State Park opened to the general public on April 27, 1936.
During World War II, the federal government purchased part of the park
in order to add land to Fort Story.[3]  In 1995 the name of the park was
changed to First Landing State Park, temporarily to be called First
Landing/Seashore State Park.[4]

Today, First Landing/Seashore State Park is still one of the most
beautiful areas accessible to nature lovers.  Because the park is located
in an area of ecological transition, the variety of plant life is extremely
large.  The park includes the northernmost habitat of some types of
flora, along with the southernmost occurrence of others.  First Landing/
Seashore State Park is a haven for botanists and other students of
wildlife, as well as those interested in geology.  With dunes, sea, and
inland waterways as its boundaries, the park area probably appears to
visitors much the same as it did to the colonists when they landed at
Cape Henry hundreds of years ago.[5]

Fifty years after these first English settlers set foot on Cape Henry,
the waters in the area were so congested that bonfires were used to
guide vessels safely through the Chesapeake Bay.  As early as 1727,
the burgesses proposed that a lighthouse be built at Cape Henry, but
taxes were high and interest waned.  Twenty years later the General
Assembly passed an act for the erection and maintenance of a light at
the cape.  The funds were appropriated by a tonnage tax imposed on
every ship that entered the Chesapeake Bay.  A thirteen-man committee was appointed in 1752 to build a tower.  This committee consisted
of able, influential aristocrats of the time, but there is no evidence that
they accomplished their task.

Another twenty years passed.  In March 1773 the act was amended
and £6,000 was appropriated to import stone for the lighthouse.[6]  In
September the treasurer of the colony, Mr. Nicholas, ordered the
materials and equipment from John Norton and Son, of London.[7]
The April 28, 1774, edition of the *Virginia Gazette* in Williamsburg
carried the following notice:

*Notice is hereby given that a number of vessels will be wanted
this summer to bring about 6,000 tons of stone from Mr.
Brook's quarry on Rappahannock and land same on Cape
Henry for the lighthouse, and the person or persons inclinable
to engage in such work are desired to treat with Matthew
Phripp, Paul Loyall and Thomas Newton, Esquire.*[8]

After the Revolution, both the first United States Congress and the
Assembly of Virginia enacted legislation specifically for the Cape Henry
Lighthouse. The Commonwealth ceded a two-acre site on Cape Henry
to the federal government, stipulating that the lighthouse be completed
within seven years.[9] The $15,200 contract was signed in 1791 by
Alexander Hamilton, federal representative, and John McComb, Jr.,
master architect.

The loftiest dune on Cape Henry was chosen for the construction site.
At this spot, it was necessary to excavate twenty feet below the surface to
find sand firm enough to support the foundation.[10] The Potomac sand-
stone, which had been quarried from Mr. Brooke's property sixteen years
before, was used to build the lighthouse. The foundation was double-
layered with rough stone bulwarks for protection against erosion.[11] At one
point, work was delayed for many weeks when almost fifty tons of sand
caved in on the excavation.[12]

The base of the lighthouse measures nearly thirty feet in diameter and
is twenty feet below ground.[13] The octagonal tower rises to a height of
seventy-two feet,[14] gradually sloping inward to a diameter of sixteen and
one-half feet at the top. It is believed that the lighthouse was operating
by October 1792, with Laban Gossigan as its first keeper. Oil lamps were
used until 1812, when an Argand lamp with metallic reflectors was
installed. A Jones fog bell was added in 1855, and a dioptric Fresnel lens,
visible for twenty-four miles, was installed two years later.[15]

During the American Civil War, the Cape Henry Lighthouse was
guarded by Union troops from Massachusetts who were later replaced by
Black soldiers.[16] In April 1861 men from Princess Anne County attacked
the lighthouse and destroyed its lamps and lens so that the United States
government could not operate them. A Union lightship was moored in the
bay until 1863, when the lighthouse was finally repaired.

In 1872 the district engineer reported that the lighthouse had become
dangerously cracked and unsafe. Six years later, Congress appropriated
$75,000 to construct a 150-foot-tall cast-iron lighthouse with a concrete
foundation.[17] The site chosen for the new tower was 357 feet from the
old one.[18] Morris, Tasker & Company, of Philadelphia, assembled the
iron work, and a brass and crystal lens was made in Paris.

## Cape Henry Lighthouses

The original Cape Henry Lighthouse was in operation by October 1792. *right* By 1872 the structure was considered unsafe. A cast-iron replacement, the tallest, fully-enclosed lighthouse in the United States, was completed in November 1881. *left*

Courtesy of the Old Coast Guard Station

In order to land equipment and supplies at the construction site, a temporary pier was erected in August 1880. However, the first freight car to venture onto the pier plunged through its planks into the water, and the pier itself collapsed just three hours after the contractors had salvaged their supplies. An investigation revealed that marine borers had eaten through the pier's foundation. As a result of this mishap, a seven-mile railroad track was constructed to haul supplies by land from Lynnhaven Inlet to Cape Henry.

The second Cape Henry Lighthouse was completed in November 1881 as the tallest, fully-enclosed, cast-iron lighthouse in the United States. The new tower was fitted with a 160,000 candlepower[19] electric light in 1923. Cape Henry became the first radio-distance-finding station in the world in 1929, flashing the letter "U"[20] (designating an "unwatched" or automatic light without an attendant)[21] in Morse code at 80,000 candlepower.[22]

In 1939 the U. S. Department of Commerce gave command of the newer lighthouse to the Fifth District of the United States Coast Guard.[23]

The original 1792 lighthouse was deeded to the Association for the Preservation of Virginia Antiquities (APVA) in 1930.[24] Today it is listed in the National Register of Historic Places and is open to sightseers.

## *Notes for Chapter* 6

1. W. H. T. Squires, "Norfolk in By-Gone Days," *Norfolk Ledger Dispatch*, 4 February 1937, 6.

2. Katherine Fontaine Syer, "The County of Princess Anne, 1691-1957," in *The History of Lower Tidewater, Virginia,* vol. 2, ed. Rogers Dey Whichard (New York: Lewis Historical Publishing Company, Inc., 1959), 66-68.

3. Louisa Venable Kyle, "A Country Woman's Scrapbook: Seashore State Park - Its Natural Beauties Have Survived Since the Days of Exploration," *Norfolk Virginian-Pilot,* 16 May 1954, part 5, 3.

4. Guy Friddell, "Park's New Name Reflects Its History," *Virginian-Pilot and the Ledger-Star,* 3 May 1995, section B, 1.

5. Syer, "The County of Princess Anne," 67-68.

6. Squires.

7. Katherine Fontaine Syer, "The Town and City of Virginia Beach," in *The History of Lower Tidewater, Virginia,* vol. 2, ed. Rogers Dey Whichard (New York: Lewis Historical Publishing Company, Inc., 1959), 124.

8. Squires.

9. Ibid.

10. Syer, "The Town and City of Virginia Beach," 124.

11. Squires.

12. Syer, "The Town and City of Virginia Beach," 124.

13. Ibid., 124-125.

14. Squires.

15. Syer, "The Town and City of Virginia Beach," 125.

16. "Gossip: Cape Henry Light Revisited by Keeper of Civil War Days," *The Tidewater Trail, Cape Henry Edition,* 1 July 1934, 3.

17. Syer, "The Town and City of Virginia Beach," 125.

18. Robert de Gast, *The Lighthouses of the Chesapeake* (Baltimore, Md.: The Johns Hopkins University Press, 1973), 13.

19. Syer, "The Town and City of Virginia Beach," 125-126.

20. de Gast, 13.

21. Gershom Bradford, *The Mariner's Dictionary* (Barre, Mass.: Barre Publishers, 1972), 286, 288.

22. de Gast, 13.

23. Syer, "The Town and City of Virginia Beach," 126.

24. de Gast, 13.

*Chapter 7*

# Early Churches

Princess Anne County was created from the eastern section of Lower Norfolk County in 1691. An act of assembly in 1695 established the existing boundaries of Lynnhaven Parish as the boundaries of Princess Anne County as well. Lynnhaven Parish, in fact, was to serve as the county's only parish for two centuries, until 1895 when East Lynnhaven Parish was formed.

Early church services in Lynnhaven Parish were held in private homes. A May 15, 1637, entry in the Lower Norfolk County records ordered that a penance of the church be carried out at Captain Thorowgood's residence. A church building was in existence by the fall of 1639, and its first recorded vestry, or governing body, was chosen the following year. The church was erected on a site called Church Point, located on Adam Thorowgood's property. At his death, Thorowgood willed the church 1,000 pounds of tobacco with which to buy "some necessary and decent ornaments."[1]

Numerous Lower Norfolk County references indicate that this first church served the community until at least 1687. In 1691 the vestry contracted with Jacob Johnson for the construction of a brick church to replace the older structure, which had begun to deteriorate. The tidal waters of Lynnhaven Bay had gradually eroded Church Point to such an extent that the site of the old church building was undermined.

A new brick church, the second Lynnhaven Parish Church, was built on a two-acre site near the road to the ferry which crossed the Western Branch of the Lynnhaven River. This land was deeded to the vestry by Ebenezer Taylor. The construction contract specified that the church building be completed by the end of June 1692 or the builder would be fined 100,000 pounds of tobacco. The contractor was authorized to make use of the materials and furnishings from the abandoned Church Point structure. This second church served its parish for nearly forty years before it was outgrown.

By August 1733 the vestry had resolved to build a larger church at Ferry Plantation, where the county already had a two-acre site for a new courthouse. Three months later, however, the vestry rescinded its previous resolution and unanimously agreed to build the new church adjacent to the old one. The new, larger church was probably built on the site of the 1695 frame courthouse, which was adjacent to the second church. The old church was converted into a public school.

Old Donation Episcopal Church, the third Lynnhaven Parish church, was accepted by the parish vestry on June 25, 1736. The first recorded reference to the name "Old Donation" appears in a vestry order dated 1822. According to tradition, the name originated in 1776 when Reverend Robert Dickson willed land adjoining the Lynnhaven church site to the parish. The bequest was to be used to endow a free school. There is little doubt that the present Old Donation Episcopal Church building is the third Lynnhaven Parish church, dating back to 1736.[2]

With the end of the American Revolution came the demise of the Church of England in America. Some ministers had remained loyal to England, while others had left the church to fight against the British. The former popularity of the church was affected by the colonists' dislike of having anything to do with England.[3] Church property was left to deteriorate until the Protestant Episcopal Church of Virginia was established in 1785.

Under the auspices of the Protestant Episcopal Church of Virginia, Reverend John G. Hull instituted a reorganization of the parish in 1842. Emmanuel Episcopal Church was built at Kempsville and Old Donation Episcopal Church was abandoned.

For forty years Old Donation remained unused, and in 1882 it was completely gutted by a forest fire.[4] To keep the church site from reverting to the Commonwealth, a religious service had to be conducted there at least once a year. Thurmer Hoggard IV and a few other stalwart parishioners made annual pilgrimages to the burned-out church to hold services. The congregation of Emmanuel Episcopal Church collected funds for Old Donation's restoration. In 1916 the parishioners' vigils were over when Old Donation was rebuilt.[5] It would not regain its former status as the "parent church" of Lynnhaven Parish until October 12, 1943, when Emmanuel Episcopal Church was destroyed by fire.[6] Old Donation Episcopal Church is located at 4449 North Witchduck Road.

Among Old Donation's prized possessions are its colonial silver communion pieces. The paten was acquired in 1711 as a gift from Maximilian Boush and is engraved with his coat of arms. The goblet (dated 1712) and the flagon (dated 1716) were given to the church from Queen Anne's Bounty. (Two years after Princess Anne became queen, she set aside for the "use of the Established Church in its poor livings, sixteen

**Old Donation Church**, rebuilt circa 1916

Courtesy of the Virginia Beach Public Library

thousand pounds a year under the name of 'Queen Anne's Bounty.'")[7]
The marble font and pewter alms basin are said to have come from the
original Lynnhaven Parish Church at Church Point.[8]

The county was also served by several smaller churches known as "chapels of ease." Since the county parish was so extensive, it was often a hardship for isolated settlers to attend the principal parish church, thus services were held at various outlying chapels. There are early references to the Eastern Branch Chapel and the Southern Shore Parish Church, both located on the Eastern Branch of the Elizabeth River.

The Eastern Shore Chapel (or "lower chapel") has offered nearly continuous service since before 1689. A court order of September 1689 called for the construction of a frame courthouse on Edward Cooper's land near a chapel of ease on the eastern shore of the Lynnhaven River. This chapel of ease, the first Eastern Shore Chapel, stood at the southern end of Great Neck at the north fork of Wolfsnare Creek. The log structure was replaced by a larger frame chapel built in November 1726 on Joel Cornick's Salisbury Plains plantation.

In October 1753 the vestry resolved to replace the frame chapel with an even larger brick structure modeled after the parent church, Old

## The Communion Silver of the Eastern Shore Chapel

The flagon, paten-cover, and chalice were made in London, circa 1759-1760, with maker's mark "WG" for William Grundy.

Courtesy of the Eastern Shore Chapel

Donation.[9] This 1754 chapel served the community until the American Civil War, when it was used as an army stable. Even though the sky blue interior was badly damaged, services were held there again in 1866.[10]

Due to an expansion of the Naval Air Station at Oceana in the early 1950s, the third Eastern Shore Chapel was razed.[11] On March 12, 1954, the fourth and present chapel was completed on a nine-acre tract on Laskin Road, with an additional eleven-acre cemetery. The pews, stained glass windows, and baptismal font were salvaged from the old chapel.[12] Like Old Donation, Eastern Shore Chapel has colonial silver communion pieces that date back to 1759. According to local belief, these communion pieces were buried in a henhouse for safekeeping because of the Union occupation during the Civil War.[13]

The Eastern Shore Chapel had as its mission the Chapel by the Sea at Dam Neck. This chapel was unique in that it was built with lumber from the three-masted barque *Agnes Barton*, wrecked in 1889 near the Dam Neck Mills Lifesaving Station. The Chapel by the Sea served its congregation until 1924, when it was bought by Christ Church of Norfolk and remodeled into a recreation camp for girls.[14]

The southern interior of the county was served by Pungo Chapel. (Pungo is a shortened version of the Indian name "Machipongo," which was also the name of the region.)[15] The first of three Pungo Chapel buildings may have been situated at the lower end of Pungo Ridge, on the peninsula between the present North Landing River and Back Bay. It was erected in this remote area as a result of a 200-acre endowment given by Captain Hugh Campbell in 1692. This endowment was for the support of lay readers in the remote parish areas of Somerton (Nansemond County), Blackwater (Isle of Wight), and North River (Princess Anne County).[16]

Pungo Chapel, the first "upper chapel" of the parish, was a frame building with no brick foundation. In March 1739 James James was contracted to replace it with a brick structure. The new site was located on William Dyer's land, which made it less remote than the first chapel. Dyer served as sexton and was reimbursed for keeping the chapel clean and for digging a well.

By June 1772 the second Pungo Chapel was in a dangerous state of disrepair and another, even larger, brick chapel was built in 1773. This chapel, built by Hardress Waller, was probably the largest church building in the Lynnhaven Parish. This last Pungo Chapel was built in the vicinity of the second chapel on a one-acre plot of land belonging to Anthony Fentress. According to George Carrington Mason, the third Pungo Chapel was probably built on the east side of Pungo Ridge Road, directly opposite the home of W. G. Eaton. This chapel declined through the years and eventually fell into ruin. The clerk of the Pungo Chapel periodically conducted services at reading places established in extremely remote areas where no chapels existed, such as Blackwater and Knott's Island.[17]

Colonial records indicate that religious dissenters also worshipped in Princess Anne County. Quakers, or the Society of Friends, were considered the "extreme left" of the English Reformation and were harassed and persecuted by local county officials.[18] William Berkeley, the royal governor of Virginia, admonished prominent county gentlemen "to have an Exact care of this Pestilent sect of ye Quakers."[19] In 1662 and 1663 over twenty people were fined for attending Quaker meetings. Richard Russell was fined for holding meetings in his house.[20]

The Quakers eventually migrated to Nansemond County and did not return to Princess Anne County for nearly three centuries. In 1954 Mr. and Mrs. Robert D. Wilson, finding no Quaker Meeting House in the area, decided to have meetings in their home. Later, with the help of fellow Quakers from North Carolina, their group built a meeting house and a school on Laskin Road.

A group of Presbyterian dissenters had a meeting house on Edward Cooper's plantation at Great Neck, near the first Eastern Shore Chapel. The meeting house was a registered place of worship by 1693. Services were conducted by Reverend Josias Mackie, who had previously been dismissed from the Elizabeth River Parish for being a radical nonconformist. By 1699 Reverend Mackie was conducting additional services at a private home in his former Elizabeth River Parish.

Baptist dissenters in Princess Anne County had their first meeting house in Pungo. John Whitehead deeded half an acre of land with an existing structure to the Baptists in July 1764. The original building was eventually replaced and named Oak Grove Baptist Church in 1856. In 1774 an offshoot of this Pungo congregation established the Blackwater Baptist Church, situated north of the Blackwater River. This church received its first permanent rector in 1803.

Following the American Revolution, the Baptist movement experienced a great revival. Eastern Shore Baptist Church was established in 1784 as a result of this tremendous growth. Its name was later changed to London Bridge Baptist Church. The original church building burned in 1946, but the congregation continues today with modern facilities. In 1835 the London Bridge congregation established a mission at Princess Anne Courthouse, which became known as St. John's Baptist Church in 1856. Kempsville Baptist Church, the fourth oldest Baptist church in Princess Anne County, was established in 1814.

Charity Methodist Church was built at Back Bay in 1789 and was the first of its denomination in Princess Anne County. It was followed in 1791 by Old Nimmo Church, a picturesque county landmark famous for its camp meetings. Bishop Francis Asbury, the first American Methodist bishop, preached there soon after it was built.[21]

In 1872 several members of Old Nimmo who were former slaves broke away from the church in order to meet in private homes. By 1873 the congregation had moved into a tiny log cabin located near Old Nimmo. The cabin was situated on an acre of land which had been purchased by the congregation from Durant Simmons for one dollar. The deed was recorded under the name of Mount Zion African Methodist Episcopal Church. A few years later the congregation built a log church, and in 1907 the present Mount Zion was completed.[22] Mount Zion A.M.E. Church is located at 2268 Princess Anne Road.

St. Mark A.M.E. Church, located at 1740 Potters Road, was also established after the end of the Civil War. The earliest worship services were held in a log cabin on land given to the congregation by E. D. Ferebee, a local resident. The original cabin burned and was later replaced by a frame building in the late 1800s. During the early 1940s, the second structure was torn down and the current church building was completed.[23]

Another quaint church was the Wash Woods Methodist Church, serving the coastal settlements at Little Island, False Cape, Sandbridge, and Wash Woods. This church was built out of cypress lumber salvaged from the cargo of the wrecked three-masted schooner *John S. Woods*, which ran aground in 1895 during a severe winter storm. The church had no regular minister. Circuit riders served the congregation until the building was abandoned in 1922.[24]

During the twentieth century, the population of the area now known as Virginia Beach has increased greatly and, as a result, has become significantly more diverse. Today, Virginia Beach is home to a multitude of churches and religious organizations representing a wide variety of denominations and beliefs.

## *Notes for Chapter* 7

1. George Carrington Mason, *Colonial Churches of Tidewater, Virginia* (Richmond, Va.: Whittet and Shepperson, 1945), 129-130.

2. Ibid., 133-139.

3. Floyd McKnight, "The Town and City of Suffolk," in *The History of Lower Tidewater, Virginia*, vol. 2, ed. Rogers Dey Whichard (New York: Lewis Historical Publishing Company, Inc., 1959), 168.

4. Mason, 147-148.

5. Katherine Fontaine Syer, "The County of Princess Anne, 1691-1957," in *The History of Lower Tidewater, Virginia*, vol. 2, ed. Rogers Dey Whichard (New York: Lewis Historical Publishing Company, Inc., 1959), 89.

6. Mason, 148.

7. Syer, 88.

8. Mason, 148.

9. Ibid., 141-144.

10. Ibid., 148.

11. Syer, 90.

12.  Louisa Venable Kyle, "A Country Woman's Scrapbook: Fourth Eastern Shore Chapel Almost Ready for Its Congregation and Their Services," *Norfolk Virginian-Pilot*, 14 March 1954, part 5, 4.

13.  Mason, 148.

14.  Louisa Venable Kyle, "A Country Woman's Scrapbook: Tossed Up by Stormy Seas, Ships That Became Chapels - Abandoned Now - These Fall Prey to Time and Decay," *Norfolk Virginian-Pilot*, 9 November 1952, part 2, 8.

15.  Mason, 145.

16.  Ibid., 149-150.

17.  Ibid., 145-147.

18.  Syer, 93.

19.  Edward Wilson James, ed., *The Lower Norfolk County Virginia Antiquary*, vol. IV (New York: P. Smith, 1951), 78

20.  Ibid., 78-79.

21.  Syer, 93-95.

22.  Mary Reid Barrow, "The History Beat: Civil War Marked Beginning of Black Churches," *The Beacon*, 8-9 July 1982, 6.

23.  Margie Hurlbut, "Old Church: Fresh Ideas," *Virginia Beach Beacon,* 28 May 1972, 2.

24.  Kyle, "Tossed Up by Stormy Seas."

*Chapter* **8**

# *Courthouses*

T he churches and the courts were the hub of the colonial community's existence. Because the Anglican Church was the Established church—that is, legally and financially related to the government—many of its functions were civic ones. These included oversight of morals, levying of taxes, care of the poor, and certification of land boundaries. When the Anglican Church was disestablished in 1784, these activities, formerly provided by church vestries, devolved on county officials.[1] Until that time the churches and the courts worked in tandem.

The early courts met in the Lynnhaven area, probably on land owned by Adam Thorowgood. In 1689 Lower Norfolk County commissioners ordered a courthouse built on the north fork of Wolfsnare Creek near the first Eastern Shore Chapel. The location at the Eastern Shore Settlement, then a thriving community, became the county seat when Princess Anne was established in 1691.[2]

In 1695 the county commissioners ordered construction of a new courthouse "upon land belonging to the Brick Church." The courthouse at the chapel was disassembled and shipped across to the west side of the Lynnhaven River. The materials were used to construct the slightly larger 1695 frame courthouse.[3] The building was to be thirty-five feet long and twenty feet wide and divided into a room for the court and a jury room. The jail was to be provided with "good posts sett so close that nor man can get through and jousts also so close and neare together and that there be stocks and pillory sett up by the court house."[4]

The next courthouse was located at the ferry which crossed the Lynnhaven River, also on the west side. This tract of land was known as "the Ferry." In 1730 Charles Smyth deeded the county two acres at the ferry for a new court building. It was to be the first courthouse in Princess Anne County to be built of brick. This site became known as Ferry Farm or Old Donation Farm and is located off Pembroke Boulevard. It

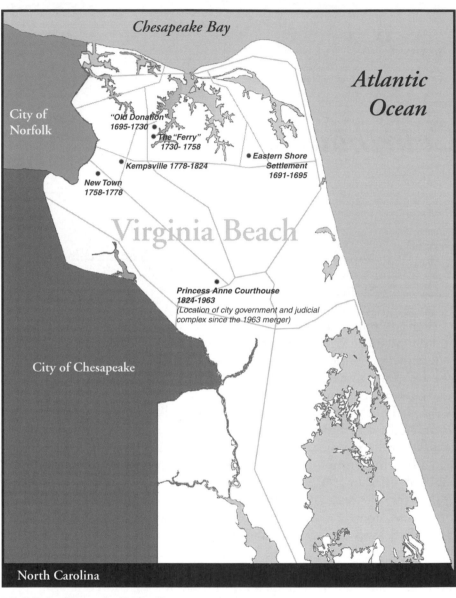

## Virginia Beach Courthouses

has been suggested that the iron bars on the existing Ferry Farm house indicate that this was the room in which Grace Sherwood was held when she was jailed.  However, that is unlikely, as the deed of the two acres for the courthouse postdates her trial.[5]

The courthouse was moved to New Town in 1758.  The village, established in 1697 on the north side of the Eastern Branch of the Elizabeth

River, was a vibrant colonial settlement. Both the Eastern Branch of the Elizabeth River and Broad Creek were navigable. New Town was a port of entry and had a customs house and a British garrison. The Walkes, the Moseleys, and other influential families lived in the area. The church

**Princess Anne Courthouse**, built 1824

Courtesy of the Sargeant Memorial Room, Norfolk Public Libraries

and court association continued as the town site adjoined Lynnhaven Parish Eastern Branch Chapel.[6]

In 1778 the court moved to Kempe's Landing, which was incorporated as the town of Kempsville in 1783. Until suitable structures could be built, the court met temporarily at George Logan's dry goods store, and his wet goods store was converted into the jail.[7] A brick courthouse and a frame jail were built. The jail burned down and was replaced in 1780 with an English bond brick structure, located behind the Peter Singleton house known as Pleasant Hall. When the county seat moved again, the courthouse was converted into a Baptist church. The jail became Kempsville Academy, a private school, and later a private residence.[8] The courthouse was demolished in 1971 after attempts to renovate it failed.[9]  The jail was in poor condition for many years and was bulldozed in 1974.[10]

The county court remained at Kempsville until 1824, when it was moved to a location at the geographic center of the county.  The area was then known as "The Cross Roads" and is now known as the Virginia Beach Municipal Center.  The commissioners entered into a contract to build the court, clerk's office, and jail.  The contract specifically noted the types of brick, thickness of walls, and kinds of wood to be used.  The contract was executed in 1820, with a completion date of 1822.  However, the court did not move from Kempsville until 1824.[11]

The Princess Anne Courthouse was subjected to so many renovations and additions that it was denied Virginia State Historical Landmark Status in 1981.  Much of the interior was deemed historically compromised and virtually only the outside bricks remained of the original 1824 building.  While denying the application, a state architectural historian noted that the "decision does not mean that the building is not of historical significance to the city of Virginia Beach."[12]  An adjacent two-story jail building, which also housed the jailer and his family, was abandoned in 1947.  It was reputed to be the site of an 1898 hanging, which was the last to take place in Princess Anne County.  A chimney collapsed in March 1964, ending a debate on the feasibility of saving the building.  The jail was demolished soon thereafter.[13]

By the 1980s it had become clear that the 1824 courthouse and its additions were not adequate for the growing city of Virginia Beach.  In 1993 a 317,000 square foot Judicial Center was dedicated.  The complex includes space for thirty-two courtrooms, court processing and administrative functions, a law library, and an underground passage from the jail to the courts building.[14]  There is the possibility that an architectural analysis of the 1824 building will occur in the future.  Perhaps there will be a renovation in keeping with the historical nature of the brick shell.

## *Notes for Chapter* 8

1.  Charles Francis Cocke, *Parish Lines Diocese of Virginia* (Richmond, Va.: The Virginia State Library, 1967), 10-11.

2.  Katherine Fontaine Syer, "The County of Princess Anne, 1691-1957" in *The History of Lower Tidewater, Virginia*, vol. 2, ed. Rogers Dey Whichard (New York: Lewis Historical Publishing Company, Inc., 1959), 55.

3.  Syer, 60.

4.  *Princess Anne Order Book*, 1691-1709, part I, handwritten copy, n.d., of entry dated 12 September 1695, 87.

5.  Sadie Scott Kellam and V. Hope Kellam, *Old Houses in Princess Anne Virginia* (Portsmouth, Va.: Printcraft, 1931), 189-190.

6.  Syer, 69.

7.  Edward Wilson James, ed., *The Lower Norfolk County Antiquary*, vol. II, (New York: P Smith, 1951) , 133.

8. Glenn Kittler, "State Landmark at Kempsville Listed for Sale," *Norfolk Virginian-Pilot*, 26 September 1948, part 3, 18.

9. Jack Dorsey, "Old Kempsville Courthouse Falls to Bulldozer's Work," *Virginia Beach Beacon*, 18 November 1971, 1.

10. Helen Crist, "Landmark Flattened by Bulldozer," *Virginia Beach Beacon*, 11 July 1974, 1.

11. Mary Reid Barrow, "Old Courthouse Set the Style: Nothing But the Best," *Virginian Beach Beacon*, 10 September 1981, 6.

12. Marc Davis, "Courthouse Is Rejected as Landmark," *Virginian-Pilot*, 30 December 1981, section D, 1.

13. Chet Paschang, "Fallen Chimney May Lead to Demolition of P. A. Jail," *Ledger-Star*, 17 March 1964, 25.

14. Marc Davis, "Beach Brings Order to Its Courts with New, Bigger, Safer Center," *Virginian-Pilot*, 10 September 1981, *Beacon,* 6.

*Chapter* 9

# War on Princess Anne Soil

THE REVOLUTIONARY WAR

The American Revolution brought civil strife to the people of Princess Anne County. Many citizens were loyal to the Commonwealth and opposed British oppression. These citizens offered their fortunes and their lives to advance the cause of independence.

The Earl of Dunmore, the last royal governor of Virginia, was in command of British forces in the Commonwealth. Early in 1775 Lord Dunmore grew anxious due to the deterioration of his power and position. On April 20, 1775, the day after the Battle of Lexington and Concord,[1] he authorized the removal of gunpowder stored in the magazine at Williamsburg. The citizens were outraged and the flames of rebellion were kindled.[2] Meanwhile, the official royal government was dissolved, and Virginia's revolutionary government, the Virginia Convention, was formed.[3]

In an effort to reassert his authority, Lord Dunmore dispatched troops to Kempsville (then known as Kempe's Landing) on October 15, 1775. Soldiers pillaged the area and destroyed the firearms stored there.[4] The local militia, known as "Shirtmen" because of their buckskin hunting shirts, engaged the British troops in combat.[5] Thomas Mathews, captain of this Virginia militia unit, was captured. He was the first patriot prisoner of war taken on Virginia soil.

On November 7, 1775, Dunmore proclaimed martial law, declaring all persons bearing arms against the British Crown to be traitors.[6] He also offered freedom to all slaves who would join His Majesty's segregated "Ethiopian Regiment."[7]

Lord Dunmore's forces were returning to Norfolk from Great Bridge on November 16, 1775. This was an attempt to fortify Norfolk for the royal government.[8] The Virginia Convention was determined that Lord

Dunmore should not hold Norfolk and ordered Virginia troops to go there and drive him out.[9] The local militia of Princess Anne and Norfolk counties assembled at Kempsville. The patriots, aware of Lord Dunmore's approach, set their troops in ambush formation. Dunmore walked into the trap.

What could have been a patriot victory, however, turned into an embarrassing disappointment. The ill-disciplined local militia fortified their courage with drink while lying in wait for the British troops. When the troops marched up, the "Shirtmen" did not attack or open fire. Instead, they fled to the woods, some soldiers being too drunk even to run away.[10] John Ackiss, a local "Shirtman," was killed on the field. He was the first Virginia soldier to lose his life in the battle for independence. Colonel Anthony Lawson and Colonel Joseph Hutchings, along with eight others, were wounded and taken prisoner.[11] Colonels Lawson and Hutchings were released the following year in exchange for British loyalist officers Jacob Ellegood and Alexander Gordon.[12] (A stone monument at the corner of Overland Road and Princess Anne Road commemorates "The Skirmish of Kempsville.")

The colonists were incensed by Dunmore's many hostile attacks, his infringement on their rights and liberties, and his seizure of their property. An ordinance was enacted by the Virginia Convention on December 1, 1775, which increased military force by directing six additional patriot regiments to be raised.[13]

The British retaliated by burning Norfolk on New Year's Day, 1776. Colonel Robert Howe removed his patriot forces from Norfolk the following month and garrisoned them at Kempsville, Great Bridge, and Suffolk. Historian William H. Stewart writes that Norfolk residents were forced "to seek shelter from the rigors of winter. The good people of Suffolk received these distressed refugees with open doors and unbounded hospitality until every building in the town was crowded."[14]

The Virginia Committee of Safety was charged with the duty of deciding the number of minute-men to be drafted in each county or borough.[15] The committee appointed the following men to serve as deputies for Princess Anne County: William Robinson, Thomas Reynolds Walker, Thomas Old, John Thoroughgood, James Henley, Erasmus Haynes, and William Wishart. These deputies were also responsible for identifying loyalist sympathizers. With a quorum of four or more deputies, a May 1776 entry in the *Calendar of Virginia State Papers* states that these men "having taken an oath before a magistrate . . . to do equal and impartial justice and to keep each other's secrets, do assemble themselves together and make strict inquiry into the temper and former conduct of the inhabitants . . . of Princess Anne. . . ." The deputies were to ascertain who supported the cause of independence, who were neutral, and who were loyalist sympathizers to the British crown.[16]

Indifference to the patriot cause should not be confused with loyalty to the British Crown.[17] To continue conducting business, merchants had to take the oath of allegiance and wear a badge of red cloth on their chests.[18]

Several local merchants were avowed loyalists. George Logan, one such merchant who chose to return to Scotland,[19] was tried in absentia on charges of treason in 1778. Logan was found guilty, and his dry goods storehouse at Kempe's Landing was appropriated for use as a courthouse.[20] John Saunders also was declared a British subject. He returned to England where he became an officer in the British Army.[21] Saunders's brother-in-law, Colonel Jacob Ellegood, was forced to leave his Rose Hall plantation. He sought security by setting up residence in New Brunswick, Canada.[22]

During the five years prior to Cornwallis's surrender at Yorktown, Norfolk and Princess Anne counties gave every indication of being a nest of loyalists. Colonel Thomas Newton, Jr. wrote to Governor Thomas Nelson that Princess Anne was

> *the enemy's country with many loyalists living in affluence,*
> *and having plenty of specie at their command, claiming the*
> *privilege of paroles, whilst the good men who left their homes*
> *are starving for want of necessaries, having no hard money to*
> *buy with and others do everything in their power to prevent*
> *the paper from passing.*[23]

Colonel William Wishart, with the assistance of Colonel Dabney, initiated a campaign of vengeance against the loyalist sympathizers in Princess Anne County.[24] The following persons were confined for treason for bearing arms against their county: Samuel Craft, Thomas Grimstead, Ethered Grimstead, Southern Cartwrite, William Hutchins, Elias Davis, Tecle Clay, and John Cooper. Rolly Grimstead was jailed for bearing arms against his county and forcing others into service. John Brown and James Weaver were also incarcerated for treasonable practices.[25] At the special local court called to try the traitors, three men could not be found to act as judges, and a near riot ensued. Although there was "sufficient proof to hang many of them if the Court was to sit here [in Norfolk]; but the witnesses have not money to bear their expenses to Richmond, & the most atrocious villians will escape. . . ."[26]

The little known Battle of the Capes, fought off Cape Charles and Cape Henry, was a major naval engagement between the French and British, marking the turning point of the American Revolution. In planning the 1781 Yorktown Campaign, General George Washington turned to French allies to supply a naval blockade of General Charles Cornwallis's British troops who were stationed at Yorktown.

Responding to Washington's request, French Admiral Francois Joseph Paul de Grasse sailed from the West Indies. His large fleet of twenty-four ships, led by the flagship *Ville de Paris*, reached the capes on August 30, 1781, and anchored in Lynnhaven Bay. British Admirals Thomas Graves, Francis Drake, and Samuel Hood appeared at the mouth of the Chesapeake with a British fleet of nineteen ships on September 5, 1781.

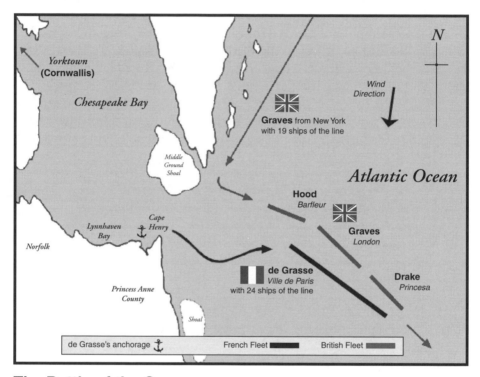

**The Battle of the Capes**

---

The British had the advantage of favorable winds and position. They could have attacked the French ships as each emerged from the Bay. Instead, Admiral Graves chose to follow traditional battle strategy and waited for the French to align themselves in battle formation. The French, however, commenced firing and heavy fighting ensued. The British suffered much more damage than the French.

After several days of extensive sea battle, the French fleet resumed the blockade, while the badly mauled British squadron limped north to New

York for repairs. This crucial battle secured American control over the Chesapeake Bay area, cutting off Cornwallis's fleet from receiving aid or escaping by sea. Trapped, Cornwallis had no choice but to surrender. The dominance of our French allies on the Virginia coast in the fall of 1781 made victory for the patriot cause possible at Yorktown.[27]

## THE WAR OF 1812

While Princess Anne County suffered civil strife during the Revolution, she escaped with only slight damage during the War of 1812. This war actually began in the waters off Princess Anne County. The United States frigate *Chesapeake* was ordered to the Mediterranean. The ship sailed from Norfolk on June 22, 1807, to relieve the USS *Constitution*. The *Chesapeake* was still undergoing repairs. Her cannons were unmounted and her crew was inexperienced. The HBMS *Leopard*, fully aware of the *Chesapeake*'s helpless condition, awaited her off Lynnhaven Inlet and followed in her wake until the *Chesapeake* halted. The British demanded the immediate surrender of four *Chesapeake* crew members. When the Americans refused, the British opened fire at close range, killing three men and wounding eighteen. The British seized four sailors, and the crippled *Chesapeake* returned to Norfolk.

The country went wild with indignation, but the diplomacy of Presidents Thomas Jefferson and James Madison postponed open hostilities for almost five years.[28] President Madison's war manifesto dated June 19, 1812, listed British violations of the American flag on the high seas, impressment of American seamen, and harassment of American vessels in their own harbors as causes for the war.[29]

After war was declared, it was assumed that the British navy would attack or blockade the ports and harbors of the Chesapeake Bay. General Robert Taylor, a Norfolk lawyer, was given command of the Chesapeake Bay's defenses and instituted a series of shore watchposts from Cape Henry to Norfolk. The British made amphibious landings near Chesapeake Beach, where they burned the watchpost and attempted a landing south of Cape Henry.[30] The county militia repelled them each time.

During the Cape Henry assault, a British frigate bombarded the coast near the area now known as Seatack.[31] Admiral Sir George Warren's fleet anchored in Lynnhaven Bay, and all ports and harbors of the Chesapeake Bay were declared blockaded on February 5, 1812. The British continued to exert their naval supremacy until the end of the hostilities.[32]

## THE AMERICAN CIVIL WAR

During the conflicts of the Civil War, Princess Anne County was spared most of the bloody ravages experienced by other southern states. For the most part, the county sent her soldiers away to war. The 20th Virginia Regiment was composed of six to eight companies of the local militia.[33] Two companies of the 15th Virginia Cavalry were also comprised of local soldiers. Company "B" was formed from the Chesapeake Light Cavalry of Lynnhaven Beach, and Company "C" was composed of the Princess Anne Cavalry.[34]

The Seaboard Rifles were organized as a state militia unit at London Bridge in December 1859. When the 6th Virginia Infantry was formed in Norfolk, the Seaboard Rifles were incorporated into it as Company "F." Company "B" of the 6th Virginia Infantry was comprised of the Princess Anne Grays.[35] The 6th Virginia Infantry saw action at numerous major battles of the war, such as Malvern Hill, the Seven Days Battles, Antietam, Chancellorsville, Gettysburg, the Petersburg Siege, and Appomattox Court House.[36]

With the advent of hostilities in 1861, only two recorded skirmishes occurred in Princess Anne County. The first occurred in April when the local militia attacked the Cape Henry Lighthouse and destroyed the lens.[37] The second skirmish occurred on October 19 when a Confederate battery at Lynnhaven Bay fired on the USS *Daylight* in the Chesapeake Bay.[38] In 1861, while General Robert E. Lee was at Rolleston in Princess Anne County, the plans for an invulnerable floating ironclad battery were formed. These plans would convert the CSS *Merrimac* into the CSS *Virginia*.[39]

Norfolk and the surrounding area were later evacuated by the Confederate forces. On May 10, 1862, Federal troops moved in and established a military district under the command of Brigadier General Egbert L. Viele (1862-March 1863) and later Brigadier General Benjamin F. ("Beast") Butler (March 1863-1864). In effect, Norfolk and Princess Anne counties were detached from the rest of Virginia and locked in solitary confinement. Martial law was imposed, personal property was seized, and the economy deteriorated. Recognized by the Federals, the "restored government of Francis Pierpont at Alexandria City"[40] enforced unlawful and extraordinary restrictions on the populace. Physicians were not permitted to practice unless they swore allegiance to the federal government. Creditors and landlords were not permitted to collect debts or repossess their property unless they had first taken the oath of allegiance to the Union.[41]

Federal forces were garrisoned at key positions around Princess Anne County. Federal troops pursued guerrilla bands, blockade runners, and smugglers pillaging the county. While the local citizens offered passive resistance to the Union forces, roving Confederate guerrilla bands incessantly harangued the Federal troops. The guerrilla harassment became so effective that Federal patrols were ordered to force half a dozen of the most influential local secessionists to act as guides to find the guerrillas.[42]

Destruction of the county's bridges was a prime guerrilla activity. In retaliation, the Federal forces issued special orders requiring that prominent secessionists in the immediate vicinity keep the bridges repaired. Bartlett Smith, Dr. Tibault, Mr. Forbes, Thomas Keeling, J. P. Keeling, John Duffey, Horatio Cornick, Henry Gournto, Martin Harris, Charles Brook, and Swepson Brook were ordered to rebuild the bridge at London Bridge within ten days, or they would be imprisoned and their personal property sold to repair it.[43]

The guerrillas had their headquarters at Fog Island. In September 1863 a force of 130 Federal troops marched on Fog Island, but the guerrillas escaped through the swamps towards Knott's Island. On September 23, while scouting Back Bay, the Federal infantry discovered a rendezvous of blockade runners. Three boats were destroyed and eleven people were captured.[44] On September 30 the Back Bay saltworks belonging to "Denis Huel, ... B. Carson, ... and a Mr. Sandis" were destroyed by Captain Kerr's Federal troops. The 100-member guerrilla force guarding the saltworks fled as the troops approached.[45]

The capture of the USS *Maple Leaf* was possibly the only Confederate engagement to occur in Princess Anne County after becoming a federally occupied military district. The USS *Maple Leaf* sailed from Norfolk in early June 1863, enroute to Fort Delaware with 101 Confederate officers as prisoners. Just outside the Virginia Capes, the prisoners overpowered the crewmen and captured the steamer. One of the prisoners, Captain Fuller, had commanded a Confederate gunboat on the Mississippi River. He now planned to sail the *Maple Leaf* to Nassau. The prisoners, however, discovered that there wasn't enough fuel for the voyage, so they beached the *Maple Leaf* south of Cape Henry and made their escape over land. Once the crew regained control of the steamer, they hurriedly returned to Fort Monroe to report the escape. Prisoners left behind during the escape due to illness or severe wounds were sent on to Fort Delaware.

The escapees pushed southward, obtaining food, directions, and advice at a remote farmhouse. They captured boats on Currituck Sound and crossed to Knott's Island, where the White family gave them food and shelter. The following day they crossed to the mainland near Currituck Courthouse, took to the swamps, and eventually met a Confederate guerrilla who guided them to Richmond and safety. In the Confederate capital, these rebels were received as heroes and were given lodging in the Spotswood Hotel, the finest accommodations in the city.

When Mr. White returned to Knott's Island, the Federal cavalrymen were not far behind him. He fled into the woods and his wife took to her bed. The cavalrymen pillaged the farm and arrested White's ten-year-old daughter for aiding and abetting the Confederate prisoners.[46] She was imprisoned at the Pungo Ferry garrison.

As the war dragged on, Princess Anne County suffered. The citizens' pre-war prosperity was nearly impossible to recover as lost fortunes were difficult to replenish in the stunted agricultural economy. The emancipated slaves lived on local farms and at Freedmen's Bureaus, which were established at Kempsville, on the Greenwich plantation, and at Rolleston, once the residence of Governor Henry A. Wise.[47] The military districts established during the war were replaced with a system of local government units in 1869.[48] Under the Reconstruction Acts, Virginia was readmitted to the Union in 1870.[49]

# *Notes for Chapter 9*

1. Rogers Dey Whichard, *The History of Lower Tidewater Virginia*, vol. 1 (New York: Lewis Historical Publishing Company, Inc., 1959), 300-301.

2. William H. Stewart, *History of Norfolk County, Virginia, and Representative Citizens* (Chicago, Il.: Biographical Publishing Company, 1902), 35.

3. Whichard, vol. 1, 301.

4. Stewart, 38.

5. Whichard, vol. 1, 302.

6. Stewart, 38.

7. Isaac S. Harrell, *Loyalism in Virginia* (Durham, N.C.: Duke University Press, 1926), 40-41.

8. Katherine Fontaine Syer, "The County of Princess Anne, 1691-1957" in *The History of Lower Tidewater Virginia*, vol. 2, ed. Rogers Dey Whichard (New York: Lewis Historical Publishing Company, Inc., 1959), 73.

9. Whichard, vol. 1, 301.

10. Harrell, 39.

11. Stewart, 38.

12. William P. Palmer and H.W. Flourney, *Calendar of Virginia State Papers and Other Manuscripts*, vol. 3 (Richmond, Va.: James E. Goode, 1881, 1890), 166-167.

13. Stewart, 35.

14. Ibid., 50.

15. Ibid., 35.

16. Palmer and Flourney, vol. 3, 166.

17. Harrell, 59.

18. B. D. White, "Gleanings in the History of Princess Anne County," in *An Economic and Social Survey of Princess Anne County*, ed. E.E. Ferebee and J. Pendleton Wilson, Jr. (Charlottesville, Va.: Michie Company, 1924), 15.

19. Edward Wilson James, *The Lower Norfolk County Virginia Antiquary*, vol. 1 (New York: Peter Smith, 1951), 9.

20. Ibid., vol. 2, 133.

21. Sadie Scott Kellam and V. Hope Kellam, *Old Houses in Princess Anne Virginia* (Portsmouth, Va.: Printcraft, 1958), 193.

22. Syer, 76.

23. Palmer and Flourney, vol. 2, 542.

24. Ibid., vol. 2, 611.

25. Ibid., vol. 2, 626.

26. Ibid., vol. 3, 101.

27. Virginia Beach Public Library, "Prelude To Yorktown: The Battle of the Capes," (pamphlet), n.d.

28. W. H. T. Squires, "Norfolk in By-Gone Days," *Norfolk Ledger Dispatch*, 11 March 1937, 16.

29. Stewart, 59-60.

30. W.H.T. Squires, *Norfolk Ledger Dispatch*, 11 March 1937, 16.

31. Syer, 84.

32. Stewart, 60-63.

33. Syer, 96-97.

34. John Fortier, *15th Virginia Cavalry* (Lynchburg, Va.: H. E. Howard, Inc., 1993), 2.

35. Michael A. Cavanaugh, *6th Virginia Infantry* (Lynchburg, Va.: H. E. Howard, Inc., 1988), 4-5.

36. Stewart Sifakis, *Compendium of the Confederate Armies: Virginia* (New York: Facts on File, Inc., 1992), 174-175.

37. Stephen S. Mansfield, *Princess Anne County and Virginia Beach: A Pictorial History* (Norfolk, Va.: The Donning Company/Publishers, 1989), 67.

38. N. E. Warriner, *A Register of Military Events in Virginia 1861-1865* (n.p.: Virginia Civil War Commission, 1959), 9.

39. "Another Scrap of History," *Norfolk Landmark*, 7 November 1879, 1.

40. Lenoir Chambers, "Notes on Life in Occupied Norfolk, 1862-1865," *The Virginia Magazine of History and Biography*, vol. 73, no. 2, April 1965, 132-135.

41. Robert N. Scott, *The War of Rebellion: A Compilation of the Official Records of the Union and Confederate Armies*, series 1, vol. 27, pt. 3 (Washington: Government Printing Office, 1889), 846.

42. Ibid., 846-849.

43. Ibid., 850-851.

44. Robert N. Scott, *The War of Rebellion: A Compilation of the Official Records of the Union and Confederate Armies*, series 1, vol. 29, pt. 1 (Washington: Government Printing Office, 1890), 143-144.

45. Ibid., 200.

46. W. H. T. Squires, "Norfolk in By-Gone Days," *Norfolk Ledger Dispatch*, 3 October 1935, 14.

47. White, 11-12.

48. Thomas C. Parramore, Peter C. Stewart, and Tommy L. Bogger, *Norfolk: The First Four Centuries* (Charlottesville, Va.: University of Virginia Press, 1994), 237-238.

49. "Virginia," *World Book Encyclopedia*, vol. 20 (Chicago, Il.: World Book, Inc., 1996), 422.

# Chapter 10

# Lifesaving Stations and Shipwrecks

B etween 1874 and 1915 more than 185 shipwrecks occurred along the Virginia coast.[1] The majority were due to rapid and violent changes in weather, which caused ships to run ashore or onto sandbars.[2] During the 1870s Congress authorized the construction of a network of lifesaving stations along the east coast in order to render assistance to ships in peril and to prevent loss of life.

Lifesaving District Six stretched from Cape Henry, Virginia, to Cape Fear, North Carolina. Five stations were built on the coast of Virginia in District Six. These were Cape Henry, Little Island, Dam Neck Mills, False Cape, and Seatack.[3] These stations served as the primary source of help for ships in distress until 1915, when the United States Coast Guard was formed.[4]

Each lifesaving station consisted of a sturdy, all-weather building with a lookout platform, a boat room, two surfboats, and various pieces of rescue equipment. The most popular lifesaving device was the breeches buoy, a cork life preserver with a pair of heavy canvas breeches attached. After an initial rope was sent to the vessel by a firing device, the breeches buoy was pulled to the ship. The endangered person would sit in the breeches with his legs hanging through and the life preserver at chest level. The lifesaving crew could then haul the buoy to safety by lines reaching from ship to shore.

Each station normally had a crew of six surfmen with a keeper in charge. Members of the crew were qualified men who lived in the vicinity of the station, manning it during the winter season, from December 1 to April 30. Each crew member was paid forty dollars per month.

At four designated times during every twenty-four hour period, two surfmen from each station would set off in opposite directions along the beach, looking for any evidence of ships needing assistance. They would

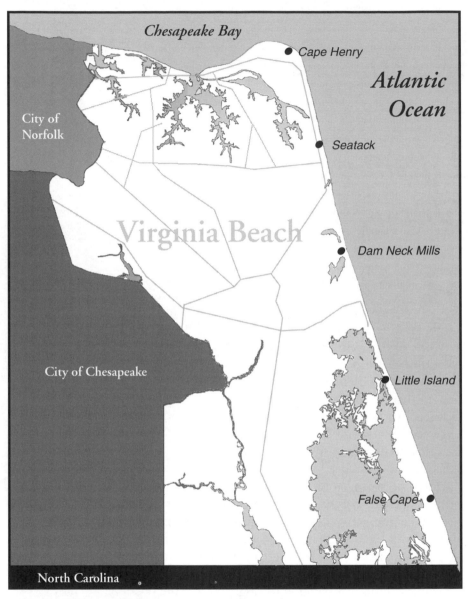

## Lifesaving Stations of Virginia Beach

meet patrols from adjoining stations, exchange information, and return to their assigned posts.[5]

The lifesaving stations also served as hospitals for survivors needing medical attention after a shipwreck. The rescued were provided with shelter, clothing, food, and other necessities. Each station had a small library of popular materials to help relieve the boredom of being stranded.[6]

## CAPE HENRY LIFESAVING STATION

One of the grandest rescues in lifesaving annals took place in 1906. According to a *Norfolk Virginian-Pilot* newspaper article dated March 1, 1906, the schooner *George M. Grant* ran aground on February 27 during a blinding snowstorm. The schooner was stranded 100 yards from the Cape Henry Lifesaving Station. Strong winds and raging seas made rescue by the lifesaving crew impossible. With darkness setting in, the ten men aboard the schooner seemed doomed to the surfmen who watched helplessly as the ship foundered in mast-high waves.

Suddenly the tug *Jack Twohy* appeared on the horizon and was skillfully maneuvered by Captain Partridge through the treacherous seas, until his crew was able to secure a line to the *Grant.* Captain A. C. Pelton and his crew of nine men were quickly put on board, and the tug then pulled clear of the schooner and headed for port.

The tugboat crew members were highly praised for their daring and bravery, but Captain Partridge modestly commented that he did no more than any other man would have done under the circumstances. He was a cousin of the Captain[7] John Willis[8] Partridge who commanded the Seatack Lifesaving Station and who, with his lifesaving crew, was standing by on shore watching the rescue.[9]

On March 31, 1906, the Italian bark *Antonio* lost her bearings in a gale and became disabled off Cape Henry. All eleven crew members were rescued by surfboat and taken to the Cape Henry station to recuperate. The bark was bound from Uruguay to Alexandria, Virginia.[10]

Fog was a major cause of shipwrecks off the coast of Virginia. It was at times so thick that navigational aides were useless.[11] On October 20, 1906, gale-whipped seas and dense fog stranded the steamer *George Farwell* near Cape Henry. All aboard were rescued. According to a newspaper account, this rescue operation involved the use of a breeches buoy as a "baggage express." Not only was passenger Frederick S. Heitmann rescued, but so was his luggage. He had been on a voyage for his health and said, after this traumatic experience, that he was "cured of the sea."[12]

## LITTLE ISLAND LIFESAVING STATION

One of the most remote lifesaving stations was Little Island Lifesaving Station, now the location of Little Island City Park below Sandbridge.[13] Tragedy struck this station in 1887. It was snowing and bitterly cold in the early morning hours of January 8, when surfmen spotted the German ship *Elizabeth* stranded several hundred yards from shore. Rescue crews rushed from the Little Island and Dam Neck Mills stations to help, but they were unable to get a line out to the ship. The decision was made

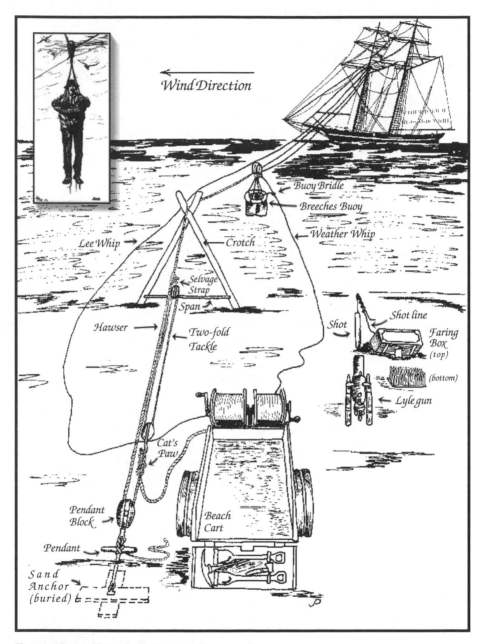

**Breeches Buoy Rescue Apparatus**
Drawing by Julie J. Pouliot

Courtesy of the Old Coast Guard Station

to risk sending a lifeboat into the raging ocean as a final rescue attempt.
The surfmen managed to reach the *Elizabeth* and took several of her men
on board. They then headed for land along with the ship's lifeboat, which
contained more of her crew members. As the two boats neared the shore,
they both capsized in the surf.[14] For days afterward rescuers pulled frozen
bodies from the sea.[15]

All members of the *Elizabeth*'s crew perished. In addition, Captain
Able Belanga, station crewmen George Stone, John Land (all from Little
Island), James Belanga, and Joseph Spratley (from Dam Neck Mills) lost
their lives.[16] They were buried at Seaside Neck, West Neck, and Pungo
Ridge. Two of the Little Island rescue party were saved. Frank Tedford
was pulled from the surf nearly frozen and semiconscious, while John
Etheridge was seriously injured.[17]

## DAM NECK MILLS LIFESAVING STATION

This station was built in the vicinity of two eighteenth-century corn
and grain windmills which operated at Dam Neck. Captain Bailey Barco,
who was in charge of the lifesaving station, bought one of the mills in
1880. The other mill was owned by David Malbon. The two mills stood
approximately 250 yards apart and were about 300 yards from the ocean.
Captain Barco's mill, severely damaged by an 1894 storm, was abandoned
and never repaired.[18]

The windmills were not Dam Neck's only landmarks. The Chapel by
the Sea, a mission of the Eastern Shore Chapel, was built there in the
summer of 1889 with lumber salvaged from the wreck of the *Agnes
Barton*.[19] This American brig ran aground near the Dam Neck Mills
station during a storm on March 14, 1889. Four crewmen were rescued
by breeches buoy before the buoy ceased moving and became unusable.
By daylight the surfmen still found it impossible to reach the ship, thus
were unable to rescue the remaining crew members before the *Agnes
Barton* sank.[20]

The *Henry B. Hyde* also became a landmark on the beach one-and-
a-half miles south of the Dam Neck Mills station. The ship went aground
twice on February 11, 1904, during a northeast blizzard. It was being
towed by the tug *Brittania*, which cut it loose to avoid being wrecked
herself. Captain Pearson, his wife, and crew were rescued. Attempts were
made to refloat the ship several times. On September 16 the *Henry B. Hyde*
was finally refloated but broke in two on October 4.[21]

Since 1951 the site of the Dam Neck Mills Lifesaving Station, the
eighteenth-century windmills, and the Chapel by the Sea has been the
property of the United States Navy.[22]

**The *Henry B. Hyde***
The ship was grounded off the Virginia Beach coast in 1904.

Courtesy of the Mariners' Museum, Newport News, Virginia

## FALSE CAPE LIFESAVING STATION

The southernmost Virginia lifesaving station was False Cape Lifesaving Station, located in the area which is now False Cape State Park. The False Cape surfmen were involved in approximately fifty shipwrecks between 1875 and 1915.[23]

One of the most memorable of these wrecks took place in October of 1889 during a tremendous storm. The *Henry P. Simmons* was sailing from Charleston to Baltimore on October 23, when her heavy cargo of phosphate rock caused her to plunge in the rough ocean and take water aboard. The schooner sank one-and-a-half miles offshore near the Virginia-North Carolina border. By noon on October 24, the False Cape surfmen and other lifesaving station crew members had been unable to get a buoy line or a surfboat to the ship. The storm raged for five days and the ship continued to sink. On October 28, as the storm abated, a surfboat was finally dispatched to the *Henry P. Simmons*. Robert Lee Garnett was the only person rescued from the ship. The other seven crew members had fallen from the ship's rigging and drowned or died of exhaustion.[24]

## SEATACK LIFESAVING STATION

Of the five Virginia Beach lifesaving stations, probably the most famous was Seatack Lifesaving Station, built in 1878 at present day 24th Street and Atlantic Avenue. The name Seatack has been traced back to a combination of the words "sea" and "attack," possibly because of a British attack from the ocean in this area during the War of 1812. The name may also have originated due to the fact that ships sailing from the Chesapeake Bay often had to tack south along the coast before heading east to Europe.[25]

The Seatack Station was a hub of growth for the Virginia Beach oceanfront resort area.[26] A new station was constructed near the site of the original building in 1903.[27] This newer building was decommissioned by the United States Coast Guard in 1969[28] and today houses the Old Coast Guard Station (formerly the Lifesaving Museum of Virginia).

Two of the most romanticized shipwrecks on the coast of Virginia Beach occurred near the Seatack Station. One of them involved the four-masted schooner *Benjamin F. Poole,* which ran aground during a gale on April 7, 1889. The ship was disabled but not ruined. Efforts to refloat her proved fruitless. The schooner rested on the beach, with Captain Charlton aboard, for seventeen months, a conversation piece for hotel guests and sightseers.

One of the sightseers was Matilda Lowhermueller, whom Captain Charlton courted and married in July 1890. They honeymooned on the vessel for three months until the *Poole* was finally refloated during a storm in the autumn of that year. The ship was repaired and remained in service for many years.[29]

Other mariners did not fare as well. The Norwegian bark *Dictator*, with the captain's wife and young son aboard, was bound from Pensacola, Florida, to England, carrying a cargo of yellow pine. She was damaged at sea by a series of storms. While heading for harbor in Hampton Roads during another gale, the *Dictator* ran aground approximately one mile north of the Seatack Station on March 27, 1891. Surfmen from both the Cape Henry and Seatack stations responded to the ship's distress.[30]

Because of a strong wind blowing toward land, the lifesaving crew's efforts to shoot a buoy line to the bark proved futile.  The *Dictator*'s captain, Jorgen Jorgensen, was finally able to float an empty barrel ashore with a line attached.  The lifesaving crew tied the breeches buoy to the line so those on the ship could haul it back.  Before anyone could be rescued, however, the buoy line became entangled in the ship's rigging and the buoy was rendered useless.  Four of the *Dictator*'s crew were able to reach shore in the ship's only usable boat, with instructions from Captain Jorgensen to send the boat back to the *Dictator*.  However, Keeper Edward Drinkwater of the Seatack Station felt that neither the ship's small boat nor a surfboat could endure the journey to and from the *Dictator* and decided not to risk sending either.  Instead, the breeches buoy was repaired and several more crew members were hauled ashore before the ship began to break apart.  Among those left on board were Captain Jorgensen, his wife, Johanne (who was near hysteria and had refused to get into the breeches buoy), and their four-year-old son.

As the ship was being battered to pieces by mountainous waves, Captain Jorgensen and Seaman Jean Baptiste, in desperation, tossed a ladder overboard in the hope that the Jorgensens could cling to it and be washed ashore.  Captain Jorgensen tied his son, Carl, to his chest and attempted to board the ladder but was swept away from it by the heavy surf.  Carl was torn from his father's arms and drowned.  Johanne, along with four others who remained aboard, also drowned as the *Dictator* was demolished.  Captain Jorgensen made the journey to shore by holding to a piece of wreckage.  Lifesaving crewmen found him later on the beach, exhausted and barely able to walk.  Second Mate Andersen also survived.

Johanne Jorgensen's body was recovered two days later, and Carl Jorgensen was found after eight days.  Both were buried in Elmwood Cemetery in Norfolk.  The heartbroken Captain Jorgensen returned to Norway following the tragedy.[31]  Years later, in 1912, he went back to sea as first officer of the Danish steamship *Pennsylvania*.[32]

After the wreck of the *Dictator*, her wooden figurehead washed ashore near the Princess Anne Hotel.  Emily Gregory, a hotel guest, spotted it in the surf and pointed it out to the hotel manager, who had it retrieved from the ocean and set up on the beach.[33]  The weathered figurehead, an elegant Scandanavian lady, stood on the oceanfront at 16th Street until 1953, when it was moved to the city garage in a state of disrepair.[34]

In 1960 Thomas Baptist, a summer resident from Arlington, Virginia, began work on a project to make the beloved "Norwegian Lady" a permanent memorial.  He appealed to the city manager of Virginia Beach and to the Norwegian Embassy in Washington.  Both received his idea with enthusiasm.  Baptist wrote an article[35] entitled "The Story of a

## Original Norwegian Lady *above*

This wooden figurehead was from the 1891 wreck of the *Dictator*.

Courtesy of the
Old Coast Guard Station

## New Norwegian Lady

*left*

The bronze statue was dedicated on September 22, 1962.

Courtesy of the
Virginia Beach Public Library

Norwegian Lady,"[36] which was well-publicized in Norway. The citizens of Moss, the *Dictator*'s home port, responded enthusiastically and raised the necessary funds to build matching bronze "Norwegian Lady" statues.[37]

Dedication ceremonies were held simultaneously in Virginia Beach and Moss[38] on September 22, 1962,[39] and the "Norwegian Lady" statues were unveiled. One stands at 25th Street in Virginia Beach and the other at the harbor at Moss, Norway, facing each other across the ocean.[40] The mission of the "Norwegian Lady" is displayed on a plaque attached to the front of the statue.

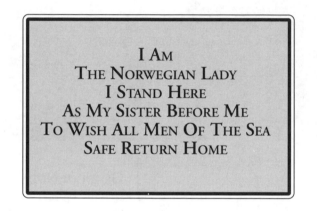

I AM
THE NORWEGIAN LADY
I STAND HERE
AS MY SISTER BEFORE ME
TO WISH ALL MEN OF THE SEA
SAFE RETURN HOME

# *Notes for Chapter 10*

1. "Early Life Savers," Supplement to *Virginia Beach Beacon*, 21-24 February 1988, B26.

2. Richard A. Pouliot and Julie J. Pouliot, *Shipwrecks on the Virginia Coast and the Men of the United States Life-Saving Service* (Centreville, Md.: Tidewater Publishers, 1986), 23.

3. Ibid., 6-8.

4. Ibid., 153.

5. Ibid., 6-18.

6. Ibid., 41-42.

7. "Crew Rescued Out of Jaws of Death." *Norfolk Virginian-Pilot*, 1 March 1906, 1.

8. Meredith Holland (grandson of John Willis Partridge). letter to Charlotte G. Irish, 27 June 1994. Courtesy of the Old Coast Guard Station, 7 March 1996.

9. "Crew Rescued Out of Jaws of Death."

10. "Italian Bark Antonio on Beach," *Norfolk Virginian-Pilot*, 1 April 1906, 5.

11. Pouliot, 156.

12. "Farwell's Crew Rescued in Darkness," *Norfolk Virginian-Pilot*, 23 October 1906, 1.

13. "Little Island Lifesaving Station," Supplement to *Virginia Beach Beacon*, 21-24 February 1988, B34.

14. "Disastrous Shipwreck," *Norfolk Landmark*, 9 January 1887, 1.

15. *Norfolk Landmark*, 11 January 1887, 1.

16. "Disastrous Shipwreck."

17. *Norfolk Landmark*, 11 January 1887, 1.

18. Louisa Venable Kyle, "Old Post Windmills of Virginia," *Commonwealth*, February 1956, 21, 44.

19. *The Dam Neck Story*, (Virginia Beach, Va.: Fleet Combat Training Center, 1988), Prepared under the direction of Captain H. E. Carroll II, n.p.

20. Pouliot, 76-78.

21. Ibid., 129-133.

22. *The Dam Neck Story.*

23. Pouliot, 160-177.

24. Ibid., 86-88.

25. Joseph W. Dunn Jr. and Barbara S. Lyle, *Virginia Beach: Wish You Were Here* (Norfolk, Va.: Donning Publishers, 1983), 19.

26. Pouliot, 155.

27. Stephen S. Mansfield, *Princess Anne County and Virginia Beach: A Pictorial History* (Norfolk, Va.: The Donning Company/Publishers, 1989), 81.

28. Ibid., 97.

29. Louisa Venable Kyle, "On the Benjamin F. Poole," *Virginian-Pilot and the Portsmouth Star*, 15 April 1956, 3C.

30. Pouliot, 94.

31. William O. Foss, *The Norwegian Lady and the Wreck of the Dictator* (Norfolk, Va.: Donning Company/Publishers, Inc., 1977), 26-42.

32. Ibid., 68.

33. Kay Doughtie Sewell, "An Old Man's Memories: Her Oldest Resident Recalls 71 Years at Virginia Beach," *Virginian-Pilot and the Portsmouth Star*, 25 March 1956, C1.

34. Katherine Fontaine Syer, "The Town and City of Virginia Beach," in *The History of Lower Tidewater, Virginia*, vol. 2, ed. Rogers Dey Whichard (New York: Lewis Historical Publishing Company, Inc., 1959), 128-129.

35. Mary Reid Barrow, "Norwegian Lady Statues: A Legacy That Means So Much to the Beach," *Virginia Beach Beacon*, 17 February 1993, 7.

36. Foss, 76.

37. Barrow, "Norwegian Lady Statues."

38. "Identical Statues Built on Opposite Shores," *Virginian-Pilot*, 15 June 1990, B3.

39. Barrow, "Norwegian Lady Statues."

40. Sam Martinette, "The Vikings Are Coming - But Just to Honor Norwegian Lady, *Virginian-Pilot*, 15 June 1990, B3.

# Chapter 11

# Virginia Beach: The Birth Of A Resort

I n the 1880s a dynamic new chapter in Princess Anne history began. Colonel Marshall Parks, a prominent developer and entrepreneur, focused local attention on the area he is credited with naming "Virginia Beach." He erected a wooden clubhouse at 17th Street which was the first structure in the area now known as the "resort strip."

Colonel Parks and his investors organized the Norfolk and Virginia Beach Railroad and Improvement Company in order to acquire oceanfront property to build a hotel and pavilion and to construct a narrow gauge railroad.[1] In mid-July 1883 railroad service from Norfolk to Virginia Beach began when Captain Virginius Freeman, engineer of the Virginia Beach Railroad, took a party of twenty-five to thirty men on the railcar's initial run. Colonel Parks's shuttle steamer service operated out of his Norfolk pier terminal and traveled the Eastern Branch of the Elizabeth River to the Broad Creek terminal. From the Broad Creek terminal, the railroad ran to the oceanfront, a distance of fourteen miles.[2]

The train brought visitors to the oceanfront area. Many visitors stayed at the Virginia Beach Hotel, a small hostelry accommodating only seventy-five guests. Located just south of 17th Street at the oceanfront, the hotel opened in the early 1880s and was financed by Colonel Parks and a group of investors developing the area into a resort.[3]

The original clubhouse was moved to 18th Street and Atlantic Avenue, where it was turned over to Mrs. Barton Meyers for use as an infant sanitarium.[4] The building was renovated and opened on June 6, 1888. Children came to the sanitarium for the fresh air and therapeutic ocean breezes as well as for free medical treatment. A nurse and a matron were hired to care for the children. The Virginia Beach Railroad offered free passes for train transportation to parents taking their children to the infant sanitarium.[5]

Colonel Parks and his associates in the railroad company did not fare well with their investments. On May 17, 1887, the hotel, pavilion, railroad, and 1,500 acres of beachfront land were put up for public auction according to a decree of the court. The sum of $170,000 was the high bid, and the buildings and property were sold to Mr. C. W. Mackey of

**Wooden Boardwalk,** 1888

Courtesy of the Sargeant Memorial Room, Norfolk Public Libraries

Pittsburgh, Pennsylvania. Mr. Mackey formerly had served on the board of directors of the Norfolk and Virginia Beach Railroad and Improvement Company.[6] Under new management and with noticeable improvements, the Virginia Beach Hotel and Pavilion reopened on June 6, 1887, for the summer season.[7]

The following year, the hotel was renamed the Princess Anne Hotel, opening for that summer season on June 1, 1888. The newspaper announcement in the *Public Ledger* called it "a magnificent hotel. . . with electric lights. . . an elevator. . . bath houses with a veranda. . . a good ballroom," among other improvements. On the roof of the hotel were three large tanks to supply water in case of a fire.[8] The fire safety equipment would become extremely important as the hotel entered the twentieth century. ·

The upgrades to the hotel made by C. W. Mackey's newly reorganized Virginia Beach Improvement Company totaled $250,000, a huge sum for 1889. A winter season, beginning in mid-February, was added to entice clientele from the north, and a New York office was opened to handle accommodations. The company also proposed to substitute standard track for the narrow gauge railroad.[9]

By 1888 the property adjacent to the hotel had been subdivided and lots were offered for sale to the public. A number of prominent citizens purchased property and began building cottages. Among the owners of the first cottages were Colonel Lucien D. Starke, Judge F. M. Whitehurst, Judge Robert Hughes, Floyd Hughes, A. S. Taylor, C. A. Woodard, Merritt Cooke, Barton Meyers, and Bishop Beverly D. Tucker.[10]

The Princess Anne Hotel stretched from 14th to 16th streets. First class bands and artists performed in the ballroom, attracting large crowds. Other amenities of the hotel included a post office, a Western Union

**Princess Anne Hotel,** circa 1907

Telegraph office, and telephone service. The hotel was praised for its healthy sea air and surf. Also, it boasted of being located at the only Atlantic beach near an extensive forest to temper cold north winds in the winter. The Princess Anne Hotel could accommodate 400 guests.[11]

Distinguished visitors and celebrities were frequent guests of the hotel, including Presidents Benjamin Harrison and Grover Cleveland and Vice-President Levi P. Morton. One guest remarked about three young people "careening madly around the dance pavilion" in describing the Barrymores—John, Ethel, and Lionel. Other visitors to the Princess Anne Hotel were Alexander Graham Bell, Cyrus Field (who laid the first transatlantic cable), and the McCormick family of Chicago, famous for their invention of the reaper and other farming equipment.[12]

Sadly, the fashionable hotel was completely destroyed by fire in the early morning hours of June 10, 1907. Sergeant Carl Boeschen of the Richmond Light Artillery Blues was hurrying to the depot to board the first train for Norfolk to attend the Jamestown Exposition. He saw smoke and flames coming from the hotel's kitchen roof and alerted the occupants. The guests escaped with only their night clothes.

The loss, estimated at $125,000, could have been much worse since there was no fire-fighting equipment at the oceanfront. A waterworks system, including hydrants and an 80,000 gallon holding tank, was to have been in operation the next day; however, these provisions were not completed in time to save the hotel. At the time of the fire, nearly twenty women residents and hotel guests formed a bucket brigade and saved surrounding buildings from destruction.[13]

Even though the hotel was a main attraction and its destruction hit Virginia Beach hard, the resort area survived and thrived. The previous year, in March 1906, the resort community was incorporated as the town of Virginia Beach.[14] Other businesses had been flourishing prior to the town's incorporation. The first grocery store opened in 1897. The store's proprietor, J. W. Bonney, was the first of the 17th Street merchants. This profitable venture was soon followed by a drugstore, a hardware store, and several general stores.[15]

Although not as grand as the Princess Anne, there were other early hotels offering modest accommodations at the oceanfront: the Ocean View, the Arlington, and the Breakers. Houses and cottages continued to spring up along the beach. B. P. Holland, a pioneer resident of Virginia Beach and its first mayor, postmaster, and telegrapher, built his second home on the west side of Atlantic Avenue in 1908. Holland had built the resort's first brick year-round home for his new bride in 1895. This house, located on 12th Street at the oceanfront, was sold to the DeWitt family in 1909. Called *Wittenzand,* a Dutch word meaning "white sand," the DeWitt household saw much activity as Mr. and Mrs. Cornelius DeWitt filled the residence with ten children.[16]

The town hall, built in 1907, housed the volunteer fire department, the first school, and the jail.[17] Thomas J. Warden was the first policeman at Virginia Beach and served as chief of police for the town.[18]

The amusement complex known as Seaside Park, spanning from 31st Street to 33rd Street, opened in 1912.  Built by Norfolk and Southern Railroad, the facility was eventually leased by the Laskin family in the 1920s.[19]  The "Old Casino," as it was called, featured a salt water pool, bath houses, a restaurant, amusement concessions, and the Peacock Ballroom.  The Peacock was "the place to go" in the 1920s and 1930s.  Charging ten cents a dance set (five or six dances) or three sets for a quarter, the Peacock Ballroom boasted such dance band greats as Paul Whiteman, Cab Calloway, Duke Ellington, and Fred Waring.[20]  A fire in 1955 destroyed most of the "Old Casino."  Seaside Amusement Park was rebuilt in the years following the fire.  A popular entertainment spot through the 1960s and 1970s, the park was sold in 1981, the attractions dismantled, and most of the property developed for motel and parking structures.[21]

The Princess Anne Country Club at 38th Street and Pacific Avenue was the resort's first country club and was incorporated in 1916.  Ninety-five acres of wilderness were donated by a real estate syndicate for a golf club and clubhouse.  Another five adjacent acres were purchased for $2,500.  The area was such a "wilderness" that mosquitoes and moccasins were a major problem in clearing the land and in the course's early years of play.  The eighteen-hole course was designed by John M. Baldwin with the assistance of Walter Becket, the professional golfer at the Norfolk Country Club.  President Harding made a historic visit to play the course in 1921.[22]

James M. Jordan, Jr., the club's youngest charter member, had the distinction of being the first man to ride a surfboard on the east coast.  Jordan's uncle, Walter F. Irvin, gave him the Hawaiian-made surfboard as a gift in 1912.  The redwood board stood nine feet tall and weighed 110 pounds.[23]

The Princess Anne Country Club added a touch of elegance and sophistication, drawing members of high society to the beach.  Affluent society was also attracted by the opening of the luxurious and exclusive Cavalier Hotel in 1927.  Located on 42nd Street and Atlantic Avenue, the Cavalier began in 1924 as a community project to foster the growth of Virginia Beach.  The Virginia Beach Resort and Hotel Corporation[24] financed the $2 million project.

When the Cavalier opened its doors, paying guests called her "the Queen of the Beach."  Governor Harry F. Byrd raved, "Virginia has the best resort hotel in America!"  The hotel boasted 226 rooms, a barbershop, a confectionery, hot and cold taps at every sink with an extra spigot for iced water, Perma-Kote washable wallpaper, a china service in the restaurant depicting the planting of the first cross on Virginia soil, silk damask hangings in the ballroom, and a 75-by-25-foot heated pool.

Famous guests included F. Scott and Zelda Fitzgerald, Fatty Arbuckle, golfer Sam Snead, Snooky Lanson, and Victor Borge.[25]

The original wooden boardwalk at the oceanfront was built in 1888 and stretched southward from the Princess Anne Hotel. Most of it was destroyed in the hotel fire of 1907. Work began on a new concrete boardwalk in 1926, when the Virginia Beach Walkway Corporation agreed to underwrite the town's $250,000 bond issue. Two wooden bulkheads were added to the concrete structure in 1938 and 1939, extending the boardwalk to the Cavalier Hotel.[26] The concrete boardwalk sustained serious damage in the Ash Wednesday storm of March 7, 1962, when twenty to thirty-foot waves battered the seawall.[27]

A unique attraction drawing visitors to Virginia Beach is the Association for Research and Enlightenment. The original building housing the collected readings of Edgar Cayce was built in 1919. It became a victim of the Depression and was sold. In 1956 the Association repurchased it. This building and the new building (housing the library and educational facility), built in 1975, are located at 67th Street and Atlantic Avenue.[28]

**Battered Concrete Boardwalk and Coast Guard Station,**
after the Ash Wednesday storm, March 7, 1962

Courtesy of the Old Coast Guard Station

The boardwalk and the resort area host a number of exciting events. The first Boardwalk Art Show was held in 1956 by the Virginia Beach Art Association, now the Virginia Beach Center for the Arts. The outdoor show and sale is the longest enduring event in the city. About 300 artists from the United States and around the world exhibit their work along the southern end of the boardwalk. The show is held in mid-June and draws crowds of over 350,000 people annually.[29]

Another tradition on the boardwalk since 1974 is the Neptune Festival, held in September. Musical performers, aerial displays, food booths, fireworks, and an art show are events associated with the festival. It has been likened to Mardi Gras, with the crowning of King Neptune each year. The Neptune Festival is listed as one of the top twenty tourist attractions in the southeastern United States by the Southeast Tourism Society. The event generates hundreds of thousands of dollars in direct taxes to the city.[30]

Since 1962 the East Coast Surfing Championships have been considered "the locals' end-of-the-summer bash." Sponsored by the Virginia Beach Jaycees, the five-day fundraising event features musical performances by national and local artists, food booths, and the surfing competition itself. Surfers from all over the United States compete in the tournament. Funds from the event are used to send children to Camp Jaycee and to assist underprivileged children.[31]

The oceanfront area of Virginia Beach is a favorite of visitors and year-round residents alike. Remembering its history as a vital and exciting vacation spot, the beach continues to be the holiday destination of numerous tourists and a beloved home to thousands of "locals."

## *Notes for Chapter* *11*

1. Stephen S. Mansfield, *Princess Anne County and Virginia Beach: A Pictorial History* (Norfolk, Va.: The Donning Company, 1989), 77-78.
2. "A Splendid Road Soon to be Opened," *Public Ledger*, 17 July 1883, 1.
3. "Marshall Parks Dead," *Norfolk Landmark*, 12 June 1900, 2.
4. "An Important Movement," *Public Ledger*, 26 April 1888, 1.
5. "The Infant Hospital," *Public Ledger*, 2 June 1888, 1.
6. "Sale of the Virginia Beach Railroad," *Public Ledger*, 17 May 1887, 1.
7. "Local Sorts," *Public Ledger*, 6 June 1887, 1.
8. "Opening of the Princess Anne Hotel," *Public Ledger*, 2 June 1888, 1.
9. "Tidewater Virginia—Its Sanitary Advantages," *Norfolk Landmark*, 20 May 1888, 1.
10. "Norfolk's Winter Resort," *Norfolk Landmark*, 13 March 1889, 1.
11. "Improvements at Virginia Beach," *Public Ledger*, 28 April 1888, 1.
12. Kay Doughtie Sewell, "An Old Man's Memories: Her Oldest Resident Recalls 71 Years at Virginia Beach," *The Virginian-Pilot and the Portsmouth Star,* 25 March 1956, C1.
13. "Princess Anne Prey of Flames: Two Lives Lost," *Virginian-Pilot*, 11 June 1907, 1.

14. City of Virginia Beach, *Reconnaissance Level Phase I Architectural Survey Report* (Staunton, Va.: Frazier Associates, July 1992), 16.

15. "Virginia Beach: Gay Arrival in Dominion Annals," *Norfolk Virginian Pilot* (75th Anniversary Edition), 1940, n.p.

16. Louisa Venable Kyle, "Old Virginia Beach Keeps Identity," *Virginian-Pilot*, 24 August 1952, Section 4, 1.

17. "Virginia Beach: Gay Arrival in Dominion Annals."

18. James J. Jordan IV and Frederick S. Jordan, *Virginia Beach: A Pictorial History* (Richmond, Va.: Hale Publishng, 1975), 84.

19. Mansfield, 122.

20. Ruby Jean Phillips, "Seaside Park Holds Many Fond Memories," *Virginia Beach Beacon Visitors Guide*, 12 August 1973, v3.

21. Joseph V. Phillips, "Seaside Park Sold: Closing in 2 Years," *Virginian-Pilot*. 2 February 81, D1, D3.

22. Kay Doughtie Sewell, "Out of a Dense Wilderness—Club and a Golf Course," *Virginian-Pilot*, 27 January 1957, C1.

23. Jordan, 109.

24. Ibid., 143.

25. William Ruehlmann, "Queen of the Beach," *Ledger-Star*, 24 June 1981, B1.

26. "Virginia Beach: Gay Arrival in Dominion Annals."

27. Jordan, 180.

28. Helen Crist, "ARE Library before Planners Tuesday," *Beacon* 12 August 1973, 1, 6-7.

29. Marlene Ford, "Now in Its 32nd Year, Art Show is Bigger, Better Than Ever," *Virginia Beach Beacon,* 18 June 1987, 19.

30. Pam Starr, "New Neptune King Learning to Be Royal," *Virginia Beach Beacon*, 17 March 1995, 4.

31. Lee Tolliver, "'Fantastic Weekend' for Surfing Bash," *Virginia Beach Beacon*, 31 August 1994, 12.

*Chapter* **12**

# Transportation

T he advent of railroads linking remote areas of Princess Anne County literally put Virginia Beach on the map. The Norfolk and Virginia Beach Railway inaugurated rail service to the beach on July 17, 1883. Norfolk and Southern took over the line in 1900. The improved railway was widened and branched to the south.

A rival railroad, the Chesapeake Transit Company, was formed in 1902. This company laid a standard gauge track from Norfolk, north to Cape Henry. The Chesapeake Transit Company's use of electric trains prompted Norfolk and Southern to modernize. Between 1902 and 1904, Norfolk and Southern replaced its narrow gauge track with standard gauge lines. Soon after, the company underwent reorganization and several name changes and ultimately became known as Norfolk Southern. Later in 1904, Norfolk Southern bought out the Chesapeake Transit Company and consolidated the single track route.

The line was expanded with trains traveling in both directions, although not at the same time, as only a single track capable of one-way "traffic" remained.[1] This was known as the loop route, creating a continuous electric loop of track from Norfolk to the resort, then back to Norfolk by way of Cape Henry. By 1906 sixteen passenger trains a day made the journey between Norfolk and the beach.[2]

A branch line ran from Euclid Junction, near today's Witchduck Road. This line continued south to Princess Anne Courthouse, Pungo, and Munden Point. The Munden Point ferry carried passengers down the North Landing River to eastern North Carolina. The line eventually was shortened to stop at Back Bay.

The southern route had several nicknames. During the week, the route was called the "Courthouse Special," because the train took lawyers to and from court sessions at the Princess Anne Courthouse. On weekends the Munden Point line was dubbed the "Sportsman's Special."

**Time-Table No. 1**

In 1897 passengers traveled from Norfolk to Virginia Beach for only 25¢.

Courtesy of Edgar T. Brown

It carried hunters and fishermen to the Back Bay area to try their luck in rural Princess Anne County.[3]  Fresh produce from the "lower country" also traveled this branch line north to be sold at markets and retail establishments.

Excursion trains ran all summer for residents who wanted to enjoy a day at the beach.  Sunday schools from all over Tidewater had their yearly church picnics at the beach pavilions of Seaside Park, Chesapeake Beach, Cape Henry, and Ocean Park.  Known as the "One-Step Special" or the "Two-Step Special" were the "Dance Trains" carrying young people to the casino for dancing each evening.

It was rare for accidents to disrupt service on the commuter line, but a few incidents did occur.  The worst accident happened on the morning of April 25, 1912, when an express train from the beach hit a freight engine.  There were no fatalities, but many of the school children and businessmen aboard were injured. A snowstorm on March 3, 1927, caused another kind of disruption in service. Passengers returning home from work in Norfolk were stranded overnight on the train which could no longer run in the deep snow.[4]

By the turn of the century, the popularity of railroads was waning, and the automobile began its reign as the supreme mode of transportation. As early as February 1904, newspapers carried stories of a spring racing tournament planned for the beachfront. New York automobile enthusiast Lee Strauss spurred interest in the coastal race, hoping to enlist

**Trolley,** circa 1920

Courtesy of the Sargeant Memorial Room, Norfolk Public Libraries

the support of other "automobilists" of the era, such as Barney Oldfield and W. K. Vanderbilt. The original course considered was a fifty-mile stretch of shoreline, beginning in Virginia Beach and extending south to Cape Hatteras.[5]

A fourteen-mile course, extending from below the Princess Anne Hotel to the wreck of the *Henry B. Hyde* and back, had been chosen for the September 5, 1904, event.[6] The Virginia Beach course was deemed even better than the one at Ormond/Daytona Beach, Florida, due to its hardness, smoothness, distance, and width.[7]

After six months of planning, the much anticipated beachfront automobile race was canceled.  Overcast skies, a blinding mist, and thundering surf along the storm-swept shore "made it evident" early in the day "that no room would be left on the beach for the automobile races."[8]

The popularity of automobiles grew from the turn of the century on, necessitating the building of roads.  In 1907 the railway was the primary means of transportation, and the only road from Norfolk to Virginia Beach was a treacherous dirt road difficult to travel.[9]  Paths graveled with shells were the first type of roads built into Norfolk, with the first concrete roads in Virginia Beach being laid in 1913.[10]

July 29, 1921, saw the opening of Virginia Beach Boulevard, the first concrete, hard-surfaced road from Norfolk to Virginia Beach.  The brief dedication ceremony drew 1,500 spectators, and 500 cars took part

**Opening of Virginia Beach Boulevard,** the first concrete road from Norfolk to Virginia Beach

Courtesy of the *Virginian-Pilot,* July 30, 1921

in the parade from Norfolk to the beach.  Flags, signs, and ribbons festooned homes and businesses along the route.  The concessions at the "Old Casino" were opened for free, and the exclusive Princess Anne Country Club welcomed the general public into their new clubhouse.  A banquet was held at the Princess Anne Country Club for the officials responsible for the opening of Virginia Beach Boulevard and the planning of the day's festivities. These dignitaries included Alex P. Grice, chairman of the committee, and John A. Lessner, president of the Tidewater Automobile Association.[11]

The 1930s brought a decline in the use of trains. The ravaging economic effects of the Depression along with the advent of the Model A Ford proved to be adversaries of the railroads. To combat the trend, Norfolk Southern bought new AFC Brill railcars and began the Norfolk-Virginia Beach Railbus in 1935. The rail buses were much like streetcars, but they were modern, sleek, luxurious, quiet, and fast. They could travel at fifty miles per hour.

During World War II, the rail bus provided the convenience of mass transit. Because of war priorities and shortages, however, the railroad could not maintain or modernize its equipment. Norfolk Southern discontinued its rail bus service in 1947. The northern and southern routes were torn up to make room for the expansion of roads in the resort area, namely the construction of Pacific Avenue. The east-west line still handles a few slow moving freight trains several times a week.[12]

Interest in a Norfolk-to-Virginia Beach commuter rail service is the subject of continued debate. A brief flurry of attention surrounded the concept of a Norfolk-Virginia Beach monorail system as early as the 1950s. The tracks of the east-west line still lie in nearly a straight line from downtown Norfolk to the vicinity of 9th Street at the oceanfront.[13] A major effort was made in 1989 to bring a light rail, trolley-type system into service by Tidewater Regional Transit and their governing organization, the Tidewater Transportation District Commission. Area city councils were divided in giving their support to the project, and the proposed light rail plan died.[14]

A 1993 study of traffic flow indicated that traffic congestion on the Virginia Beach-Norfolk Expressway and Interstate 264 had reached serious levels. Transportation experts say that traffic volume on the expressway is projected to increase by 87 percent by the year 2015. One million dollars was appropriated in January 1995 to re-examine the traffic problem, possibly leading to a reconsideration of a light rail system serving Hampton Roads communities.[15]

A major feat of engineering is located in the Bayside area of the city. The Chesapeake Bay Bridge Tunnel, which opened April 15, 1964, took 3½ years and $200 million to build.[16] The 17½ mile combination of trestles, bridges, and tunnels links Chesapeake Beach to Wise Point on the Eastern Shore.[17] The Chesapeake Bay Bridge Tunnel is well traveled, with an average count of over 7,500 vehicles per day.[18]

# *Notes for Chapter* *12*

1.  Brown Carpenter, "Dead Beach Rail Links Recalled," *Ledger-Star*, 25 January 1974, A7.
2.  Carl Craft and Nell Craft, "When Trains Made Tracks for the Beach," *Virginian-Pilot*, 27 July 1975, C5.
3.  *Ledger-Star*, 25 January 1974, A7.
4.  *Virginian-Pilot*, 27 July 1975, C5.
5.  "Lee Strauss, the Well-Known New York Enthusiast, Is in Town and Will Meet Virginia Sportsmen This Afternoon," *Virginian-Pilot*, 12 February 1904, 12.
6.  "Autos Will Speed on Beach for Trophies," *Virginian-Pilot*, 4 September 1904, 12.
7.  *Virginian-Pilot*, 12 February 1904, 12.
8.  "Celebration at Virginia Beach," *Virginian-Pilot*, 6 September 1904, 2.
9.  Pat Roebuck, "Gettel Remembers Beach Progress in Terms of Days Railroading," *Beacon*, 30 July 1970, 23.
10.  "Virginia Beach: Gay Arrival in Dominion Annals," *Norfolk Virginian-Pilot*, (75th Anniversary Edition), 1940, n.p.
11.  "500 Automobiles in Parade Opening VA Beach Road," *Virginian-Pilot*, 30 July 1921, 14.
12.  *Ledger-Star*, 25 January 1974, A7.
13.  Jim Henderson, "Revival of Beach-Norfolk Commuter Rail Sought," *Virginian-Pilot*, 9 August 1971, B1.
14.  Mike Knepler, "Councils Track Future of Light Rail," *Virginian-Pilot*, 19 February 1989, B1.
15.  Mac Daniel, "Study Will Consider Norfolk-to-Beach Light-Rail Possibility," *Virginian-Pilot*, 27 January 1995, B5.
16.  Nigel Hawkes, *Structures: The Way Things Are Built* (New York: Macmillan Publishing Company, 1990), 232
17.  Don Hill, "Traffic Rolls Across Bay," *Virginian-Pilot*, 16 April 1964, 1, 10.
18.  Staff, Accounting Department, Chesapeake Bay Bridge Tunnel District, telephone interview by author. Virginia Beach, Va., 7 February 1996.

*Chapter 13*

# The Military

Although no bombs fell on Hampton Roads during the two world wars, the fear of war was an ever present reality. The natural terrain of Tidewater, the Chesapeake Bay, and the surrounding waterways contributed to the establishment of military forces in the area.

Military aviation began on the Tidewater peninsula in the early 1920s. Test bombings were conducted to evaluate battle attack readiness over the summer of 1921. In July of that year, aviators sank former German warships the *Frankfort* and the *Ostfreisland* in joint army and navy exercises off the Virginia Capes. Scores of military and national government officials witnessed these tests of potential air power.[1]

Twenty years later, the escalation of World War II and the increased need for air bases prompted the navy to acquire a 330-acre tract of land near Oceana for an auxiliary airfield.[2] In February of 1941, 272 acres near Creeds was acquired for an additional airfield.[3] One month later a third tract of land, 441 acres northeast of Pungo, was obtained for naval airplane landing sites.[4]

With the anticipation of war, military personnel, defense workers, and their families poured into the area. By the end of 1940, the only homes available were unheated cottages at the beach, and the housing situation only got worse.[5]

The State Planning Board, in cooperation with the Hampton Roads Defense Council, conducted a housing survey in the area from April 1940 to May 1941. Results indicated that the population of the southside, including Norfolk and Princess Anne County, had increased by 23 percent.[6] To help cope with the housing shortage, the navy commandeered several resort hotels, including the Cavalier and the Nansemond, for the duration of the war.[7] The Tidewater Hotel Association advertised in out-of-town newspapers for tourists to stay at home until the war ended. The area was subject to blackouts, the beaches were closed after dark, and guest rooms were not available.[8]

Visitors were discouraged by the threat of the enemy lurking off the waters of the coast. German submarines operating off Cape Henry sank eight vessels in 1942 alone.[9] Oil slicks and debris continually washed ashore. On the afternoon of June 15, 1942, crowds of beachgoers heard an underwater explosion and witnessed two tankers sinking five miles from shore.[10] The last reported submarine attack off Cape Henry occurred on April 18, 1945, with the sinking of the steamship *Swiftscout*.[11]

Today, four military installations are based in Virginia Beach. They are located at Fort Story, Oceana, Dam Neck, and Little Creek. The oldest and most historic of these is Fort Story.

## FORT STORY

In the early 1900s, citizens and businessmen believed that a military installation was needed at Cape Henry as a first line of defense against an attack. Henry T. Trice, secretary of the Virginia Industrial Commission, proposed studies to convince the War Department and the federal government that "billions of dollars worth of property lying in an unprotected state within the Virginia Capes" could be easily accessed "by an enemy in time of hostilities."[12] In 1913 President William Howard Taft signed an appropriations bill to purchase land at Cape Henry. The $8 million facility was named for General John P. Story, a Virginia-born general and artillery expert.[13]

During World War I, Fort Story was called "the American Gibraltar" and once was considered to have the heaviest armament of any fort on the Atlantic Coast.[14] Soon after it was established, the fort expanded as additional acreage was acquired through the purchase of condemned properties around the facility. In 1940 the War Department granted the army use of 694 acres of Seashore State Park, inciting protests from civilians, scientists, and nature lovers. Outrage rang out at the army's apparent violation of the park's virgin wilderness.[15] Also angering many citizens was the beachfront location of the fort's hospital. The hospital site was moved inland to save the shore's natural features and scenery.[16]

Fort Story's varied terrain provided excellent training grounds. Beginning in 1940, the facility served as a training site for World War II soldiers.[17] At one time, Fort Story was the location of a NIKE-Hercules guided missile site.[18] Scenic Fort Story also features the Cape Henry Memorial Cross which was erected in 1935. The cross marks the place where Jamestown settlers first arrived in the area on April 26, 1607.[19] The first lighthouse authorized by the federal government sits at Fort Story. It began operation

## World War II - Fort Story
Photo by H. D. Vollmer, 1944

Courtesy of the Sargeant Memorial Room, Norfolk Public Libraries

in 1792 and remained a vital beacon until 1881, when a new Cape Henry lighthouse was completed.

The fort is still a very active facility today. Approximately 4,000 active duty personnel, their dependents, and civilian employees currently call Fort Story home.[20]

## OCEANA

Plans for another Virginia Beach installation, the Oceana Air Station, began as early as 1938. Investigations into building an auxiliary landing field on acreage near Oceana and Princess Anne Courthouse were conducted. Construction began in 1941 with a 2,500-foot runway and a wood-frame building, which served as an ambulance garage and caretaker's office.

The attack on Pearl Harbor stepped up construction deadlines and provided impetus for building better facilities. The station was commissioned on August 17, 1943, and remained in active status through World War II and the Korean War. In 1950 an expansion extended four runways to 8,000 feet, making the facility a master jet base. The station was designated a naval air station on April 1, 1952, and officially was dedicated as Naval Air Station Oceana in June 1957.[21]

NAS Oceana began over fifty years ago on 328 acres of swampland. It has now grown to 5,000 acres with 15,000 active duty personnel, their families, and civilian employees.[22] Pentagon plans for NAS Oceana's expansion will result in over 5,000 additional personnel in the next few years.[23]

**F-14 Tomcat**
A fighter, based at NAS Oceana, flies over the Virginia Beach oceanfront.

Courtesy of the Public Affairs Office, Naval Air Station (NAS) Oceana

## DAM NECK

In the southern part of the city is the military facility Dam Neck, named for a lifesaving station established on that spot in the late 1800s. At that time, the site was a deserted beach near two post-type grain windmills known as Dam Neck Mills. Called the Fleet Air Defense Training Center,

Dam Neck was first organized as an anti-aircraft school in the beginning of World War II. Later, it was increased in size to accommodate Korean War operations. Military personnel are trained in the operation and maintenance of missiles at Dam Neck's Naval Guided Missiles School.[24]

The Dam Neck facility is known officially as the Atlantic Fleet Combat Training Center and covers nearly 1,200 acres. Around 5,800 active duty personnel, their family members, and civilian employees are located at Dam Neck.[25]

## LITTLE CREEK

The navy began building the Amphibious Training Base at Little Creek in April 1942. Construction of the base was a concentrated effort. Five buildings a day were completed on a water-logged bean field. The mud and adverse conditions allowed for drills focused on new methods and techniques in assault landings. These maneuvers perfected the capturing of enemy land featuring difficult terrain.

The Amphibious Training Command, U.S. Atlantic Fleet, officially began operation on August 1, 1943. Functioning under the auspices of Little Creek were the Naval Frontier Base, Camp Bradford, and Camp Shelton. The Amphibious Training Command at Little Creek trained over 200,000 naval and 160,000 army and marine personnel in World War II. When the war ended, the command was deactivated, and the

**Tidewater Veterans Memorial,** built 1988

Courtesy of the Virginia Beach Public Library

United States Naval Amphibious Base was created. Congress allocated funds for developing and improving the facility in the early 1950s.[26]

Now a part of the Norfolk Naval Base, Little Creek Naval Amphibious Base is a component of the largest naval installation in the world.[27] Little Creek numbers over 11,600 active duty military personnel and approximately 3,000 civilian employees.[28]

In 1988 South Hampton Roads' first monument to all United States war veterans was built. The thirty-five foot structure is located on Pavilion Drive near the oceanfront. The memorial, costing $500,000, was six years in the making and was constructed from the designs of three Virginia Beach students. On dedication day, Congressman Owen Pickett stated that the Tidewater Veterans Memorial "will stand always as a solemn reminder of the high price of freedom and liberty."[29]

## Notes for Chapter *13*

1. "Aircraft Attack Fails in Attempt to Sink Warship," *Norfolk Virginian-Pilot*, 21 July 1921, 1.
2. "Navy Acquires Princess Anne Landing Field," *Norfolk Virginian-Pilot*, 19 December 1940, 22.
3. "U.S. Acquires Creeds Land for Airfield," *Norfolk Virginian-Pilot*, 6 February 1941, 20.
4. "New Air Field, 441 Acres, for Navy at Pungo," *Norfolk Virginian-Pilot*, 21 March 1941, part 2, 14.
5. Marvin W. Schlegel, *Conscripted City: Norfolk in World War II* (Norfolk, Va.: Norfolk War History Commission, 1951), 31.
6. Ibid., 59.
7. Ibid., 361.
8. Ibid., 350.
9. Edward Rowe Snow, *Famous Lighthouses of America* (New York: Dodd, Mead & Company, 1955), 165-166.
10. Schlegel, 191.
11. Snow, 165-167.
12. "Map to Set Forth Need of Fortifications at Capes," *Virginian-Pilot*, 29 December 1909, 3.
13. Stephen S. Mansfield, *Princess Anne County and Virginia Beach: A Pictorial History* (Norfolk, Va.: The Donning Company/Publishers, 1989), 106.
14. James M. Jordan IV and Frederick Jordan, *Virginia Beach: A Pictorial History* (Richmond, Va.: Hale Publishing, 1974), 105.
15. "State Commission Receives Numerous Protests against Army Using Seashore Park," *Norfolk Virginian-Pilot*, 29 September 1940, part 2, 1.
16. "Fort Story Hospital Site is Relocated," *Norfolk Virginian-Pilot*, 5 October 1940, 16.
17. Schlegel, 20.
18. Rogers Dey Whichard, *The History of Lower Tidewater Virginia*, vol. 2 (New York: Lewis Historical Publishing, Inc., 1959), 119.
19. Jordan and Jordan, 14-15.
20. Dan Cragg, *Guide to Military Installations*, 4th ed. (Mechanicsburg, Pa.: Stackpole Books, 1994), 297.
21. Whichard, 103-104.
22. Cragg, 305.
23. Jack Dorsey and Dale Eisman, "Ocean Comes Out a Winner," *Virginian-Pilot*, 1 March 1955, A1.
24. Whichard, 104.
25. Cragg, 301.
26. Whichard, 102-103.
27. Cragg, 302.
28. *Polk 1995 Virginia Beach, Virginia, City Directory* (Richmond, Va.: R. L. Polk, 1995), 5-6.
29. Lamar B. Graham, "Veterans Gather to Remember, Dedicate Memorial," *Virginian-Pilot*, 31 May 1988, D1, D3.

Chapter *14*

# *The Merger*

P rincess Anne County land adjacent to the city of Norfolk rapidly became suburbanized. In the 1950s Norfolk was extending city waterlines far out into the county to service the developing subdivisions. Princess Anne County and the city of Virginia Beach were dependent on Norfolk for their water supply. It was reasonable to assume that territorial claims eventually would follow the boundaries of Norfolk's waterlines.[1]

Traditionally, unincorporated county territory bordering an incorporated city was subject to municipal annexation. As county land adjacent to Norfolk became less rural and more urban in character, the city was allowed to annex such areas to accommodate urban growth. According to state laws, annexation claims were decided solely on the basis of orderly growth and development of the entire area, rather than the wishes of the residents. No provisions were made for a referendum by the city, county, or the area proposed for annexation.[2]

## ANNEXATION PROBLEMS

On January 1, 1959, Norfolk became the eighth largest city in the south by annexing 13½ square miles of Princess Anne County, which was home to 38,000 residents.[3] The politics of Princess Anne County and Virginia Beach were dominated by Sidney S. Kellam.

Kellam's family was prominent in both the political and civic affairs of the community. His father, Abel Kellam, was clerk of the circuit court of Princess Anne County for twenty years, and his brother, Floyd Kellam, was the circuit court judge. Sidney Kellam learned the techniques of politics firsthand, and in 1931 he was elected county treasurer. He ran for treasurer unopposed four more times, headed the Department of Conservation and Economic Development, and served eight years on Virginia's

Democratic National Committee.  The Kellam organization was perhaps
the strongest local political machine in Virginia.  The organization was
cohesive, well disciplined, and supported by the most influential segments
of the community.[4]

The Kellam organization clearly recognized that Norfolk's annexations
were likely to continue.  To stop further annexation, the organization
leaders lobbied unsuccessfully during Virginia's 1960 General Assembly
to have the state's annexation law modified to protect Princess Anne
County's territorial integrity.

Their lobbying prompted Norfolk to delay any further extension of
water service into Princess Anne County.  Water was a key factor in the
growth of both the city and county.  Suburban tract developers were so
enraged by the delay that Kellam appeared before the Norfolk City
Council in April 1960 with a proposal for a five-year moratorium on
annexation procedures against Princess Anne County.  Kellam agreed
not to lobby in the Virginia General Assembly for any changes in the
state annexation laws.  Also proposed was the appointment of a special
joint committee to study the possibilities of "a metropolitan government"
in Tidewater.[5]  A seven-man committee was formed, with Kellam named
as chairman.[6]

## CONSIDERING CONSOLIDATION

Kellam's maneuvering had gained the county some needed time in
diverting Norfolk's attention from annexation.  When on October 3, 1961,
Virginia Beach and Princess Anne County publicly announced their intent
to study merger possibilities, Norfolk city officials were taken by surprise.[7]
In a newspaper advertisement on October 28, 1961, the Norfolk City
Council stated their belief that "the proposed merger will not be helpful
to the present progressive vitality of the Tidewater area or beneficial to the
individual citizens of Princess Anne County or Virginia Beach."[8]

The threat of annexation by Norfolk was becoming very real for the
county residents.  Norfolk Mayor W. F. Duckworth hinted at possible repercussions to the residents of Princess Anne County.  Duckworth stated if the
city of Norfolk was prevented permanently from the normal, healthy expansion of most progressive cities, the citizens could be justifiably resentful.[9]

On December 5, 1961, the Norfolk City Council voted to cut off
water service to areas of Princess Anne County if the voters ratified the
merger.  Although Mayor Duckworth and the city council refused to
acknowledge the vote as a challenge, the county residents saw it as a threat.
Earl W. Kingsbury, a representative of the Aragona Civic League, raged,
"They are squirting a water pistol at us.  Let's merge."[10]

## The Merger Campaign

The merger was a well-planned, well-executed political campaign, conducted by Sidney Kellam's Consolidation Study Committee. Members of the committee were R. Lee Bonney, Clayton Q. Nugent, R. L. Riggs, Frank E. Dickerson, A. L. Bonney, Alton Williams, Charles Burlage, J. W. Wood, D. L. Gregory, and N. C. Chandler. In October 1961 Kellam stated, "I'm confident that Princess Anne County is going to find some way to become a city." The key to the merger proposal was the county's desire to forestall any further annexations by Norfolk.[11]

By the end of October, the committee outlined consolidation problems, settled on the name of Virginia Beach, resolved joint political representation, and assessed the city and county indebtedness. The name "Virginia Beach" was approved because it was considered to be better known, particularly in business and tourist advertisements. The name "Princess Anne" was retained by renaming the Seaboard Magisterial District "the Princess Anne Borough." The principal seat of government was to be located at the Princess Anne Courthouse and became known as the Virginia Beach Municipal Center.

The respective elected officials decided the details for a city council-type representation among themselves. It appears that there were no consistent methods or criteria for deciding who would be the principal and/or the deputy officials in the consolidated city government structure. Thus, the county's board of supervisors and the city's councilmen all became members of the consolidated city council.[12]

The Richmond law firm of Hunton, William, Gay, Powell, and Gibson was retained to draw up a working charter and a consolidation agreement.[13] On November 4 the charter was presented to the public and endorsed by the Virginia Beach Chamber of Commerce. The Virginia Beach City Council and the Princess Anne Board of Supervisors unanimously approved the merger agreement and charter on November 10, 1961.[14]

The next step was to win acceptance at the polls on January 4, 1962. The referendum was the end result of a well organized political campaign carried to voters on a direct, personal, small group basis. Elected public officials were promoting the merger. Many of the people active in the initial phases of the proposed consolidation joined the campaign as members of the Speakers Bureau. They spoke to civic groups, women's clubs, church organizations, government classes, and even school assemblies. Public officials led rallies, were principal speakers, and served as "authorities" on the merger. Being familiar with local government and their specific offices, these officials were able to present in detail what effects the merger would have on the individual citizen.[15] Throughout November and December, virtually every organized group in Princess Anne County and Virginia Beach heard a presentation from a pro-merger speaker.[16]

Although little local opposition was voiced, several pointed questions were directed to the pro-merger leaders. In addition, a few letters to the editor appeared in the local newspaper. Opposition was strongest in the affluent areas near the resort city, such as Bay Colony, North Virginia Beach, and Birdneck Point. These residents had strong financial and emotional ties to Norfolk.[17]

In a final attempt to delay the referendum, Littleton B. Walker, a longtime Kellam foe, filed suit against the City of Virginia Beach and the County of Princess Anne, challenging the constitutionality of the merger. The case was not decided until April 17, 1962, several months after the referendum, when Walker's suit was dismissed and no appeal was made. Kellam had labeled the action "political propaganda filed under the guise of a legal suit." Kellam further accused Walker of "spending hundreds of dollars to run newspaper ads in an effort to confuse the people."[18]

The outcome at the polls never appeared to be in doubt. The voters overwhelmingly approved the merger. The official tabulation in Virginia Beach was 1,539 for and 242 against. In Princess Anne County the count was 7,476 for and 1,759 against.[19] The predominantly Black precinct of Seatack led all the polling places by a whopping 22-1 margin in favor of the merger. Anti-merger forces did not carry a single precinct. The lowest margin of victory was Cape Henry precinct with a 3-2 margin.[20] The people had spoken. The merger campaign was over.

## THE CITY CHARTER AND THE GENERAL ASSEMBLY

After voter approval of the merger, the leadership focused on getting the merger charter passed by the General Assembly. V. A. Etheridge, treasurer of Virginia Beach, took up temporary residence in the Hotel Richmond to see the charter bill through this process.[21] Actually, Virginia Beach politicians had begun to lobby well in advance of the General Assembly session. During the preceding fall gubernatorial election, they had backed the state Democratic organization candidate and had produced organization majorities at the polls. Norfolk voters, on the other hand, failed to support the state organization candidates. As a result, in an "organization-dominated" 1962 General Assembly, there was little sympathy for Norfolk when Virginia Beach's charter bill came before the assembly.

For Virginia Beach it was simply a matter of collecting the rewards. The General Assembly handled the charter as a routine matter. They viewed the consolidation as being local in nature, an important factor in

**Sidney Kellam,** voting in the 1962 referendum

Courtesy of the *Virginian-Pilot* and the *Ledger-Star*. Supplement to the Virginia Beach *Beacon*, February 21, 1988

legislative thinking. They also accepted the "pro-mergerites'" tenet that the merger would enhance, not stifle, future metropolitan cooperation.[22] The House of Delegates overwhelmingly approved the merger charter by a vote of 85 to 9.[23] It was approved and enacted by the General Assembly on February 28, 1962. The consolidation of the City of Virginia Beach and Princess Anne County would become effective on January 1, 1963.

## THE TRANSITION

Once the charter was ratified, the transitional phase of the consolidation began. The transition lasted less than a year and went smoothly due to two factors. Both Virginia Beach and Princess Anne County had a history of certain shared functions and officers. Joint functions included schools, health, welfare, library service, and mosquito control. The joint officers were the school superintendent, the clerk of the circuit court, and the Commonwealth's attorney. The second factor was the dominance of the Kellam organization in both city and county affairs. The organization provided a unified political framework and approached transition as a group effort.

The existing Merger Executive Committee coordinated transition activities. This committee was headed by Ivan Mapp, the county commissioner of revenue, and included the county clerk of the circuit court, county treasurer, city treasurer, city commissioner of revenue, and city sergeant. The Merger Executive Committee met in joint sessions with the city council and the county board of supervisors.

Between March and November 1962, numerous special committees were appointed to study and to make recommendations on particular aspects of the consolidation. They included the Committee on Street Names and Numbers, the Committee on Equalization of Tax Assessments, the Water Committee, the Transportation Committee, the Committee to Study Garage Facilities, the Committee on Ordinances, the Committee to Decide Office Locations, the Committee to Negotiate for the Purchase of Land, and the City Seal Committee.

In addition to the recommendations of these special committees, the Merger Executive Committee requested reports from city and county officials. These reports were compiled in order to identify problems and to define operational limits, functions, and responsibilities of the consolidated city departments.

By September 1962 most of the problems had been identified and attention turned to the actual setting up of the new city government. Numerous appointments were announced. Operational plans were finalized for the offices of commissioner of the revenue, treasurer, and high constable, and the city manager's salary was fixed. A legal publishing firm was engaged. Special taxes on amusements, food, lodging, and cigarettes were approved. Miscellaneous decisions on matters such as the slogan "World's Largest Resort City" were made.

The final joint session of the Merger Executive Committee and the two governing boards (one for the city, one for the county) took place on December 28, 1962. The City of Virginia Beach became a reality on January 1, 1963.[24]

## THE CITY OF VIRGINIA BEACH

The charter of the consolidated city provided for a council/city manager form of government. Virginia Beach was divided into seven boroughs. The city which existed prior to the merger became the Virginia Beach Borough. The six remaining boroughs, Bayside, Blackwater, Kempsville, Lynnhaven, Princess Anne (formerly Seaboard), and Pungo, were the former six magisterial districts of Princess Anne County.

Eleven elected council members representing the seven boroughs comprised the city council. By a majority vote the council selected one among them to be mayor and one to be vice-mayor. (The mayor became a position elected by popular vote in 1988.)[25] The mayor presided over council meetings and acted as the ceremonial head of city government. The vice-mayor assumed the mayoral duties in the absence of the mayor. The city council appointed the city manager, who was the executive and administrative head of the city government. Hiring the city manager was based on executive and administrative qualifications.[26]

In its first formal meeting held on January 1, 1963, the city council appointed the city manager, clerk, city attorney, welfare board, and police and fire trials board. The council also adopted twenty-seven city ordinances. At the meeting a mahogany plaque with a bronze copy of the official City Seal was presented to Mayor Frank A. Dusch.[27] The seal was designed by Mrs. H. Ashton Williamson, Jr. of Oak Grove. It bears the motto "Landmarks of Our Nation's Beginning" and depicts the Cape Henry Lighthouse and the First Landing Cross on a sunlit beach. This scene is surrounded by an inner ring of strawberry leaves and an outer ring of leaping marlins.[28] A group of navy men aboard the USS *Amphion* made the bronze replica, and it was presented by Captain Joseph W. Crawford, Jr.[29]

The City of Virginia Beach as we know it today continually grows in population and sophistication. In 1963 nearly 37 percent of the total acreage of the city was farm land, which outranked all the state's counties in yield per acre of corn and wheat.[30] However, the rural character that predominated in 1963 rapidly faded. The huge county farms gave way to subdivisions, office parks, shopping centers, and planned residential communities.

## Notes for Chapter 14

1. Luther J. Carter, "Borough Offered by P. A.," *Virginian-Pilot*, 4 April 1960, 1, 5.

2. David G. Temple, *Merger Politics: Local Government Consolidation in Tidewater Virginia* (Charlottesville, Va.: University of Virginia Press, 1972), 17.

3. Gene Roberts, "Norfolk Becomes Eighth City in the South, Population-Wise," *Virginian-Pilot,* 1 January 1959, 36.

4. Temple, 39-41.

5. Ibid., 74.

6. "First Ripples of Metropolitan Study," *Virginian-Pilot,* 13 August 1960, 4.

7. "Merger Study Asked," *Virginian-Pilot*, 3 October 1961, 17.

8. George M. Kelley, "Norfolk Brands Merger as Progress Threat," *Virginian-Pilot*, 29 October 1962, 1.

9. Temple, 77.

10. Frank R. Blackford, "Beach-P.A. Merger Move Expected Monday," *Virginian-Pilot*, 4 November 1961, 1, 3.

11. William E. Tazewell, "Consolidation Study Committee Appointed," *Virginian-Pilot*, 5 October 1961, 31.

12. *Virginian-Pilot,* 4 November 1961, 1, 3.

13. Princess Anne—Virginia Beach Merger Committee Papers. Central Library Archives. Virginia Beach, Virginia.

14. *Virginian-Pilot*, 11 November 1961, 1.

15. Temple, 72.

16. Ibid., 80.

17. Frank R. Blackford, "Suburbia Shakes Old Norfolk Ties," *Virginian-Pilot*, 4 December 1961, 17.

18. Temple, 78-79.

19. Ibid., 82.

20. Frank R. Blackford, "Beach-P.A. Merger Wins by Sweeping 5-1 Margin," *Virginian-Pilot*, 5 January 1962, 1.

21. Temple, 99.

22. Ibid., 102-103.

23. George M. Kelley, "P.A.-Beach Charter Passes House, 85 to 9," *Virginian-Pilot*, 2 February 1962, 1.

24. Temple, 22-126.

25. Stephen S. Mansfield, *Princess Anne County and Virginia Beach: A Pictorial History* (Norfolk, Va.: The Donning Company/Publishers, 1989), 13.

26. "Charter for the City of Virginia Beach,"*Virginian-Pilot*, 16 November 1961, 40.

27. Temple, 126.

28. Frank R. Blackford, "Housewife Designs New Beach Seal," *Virginian-Pilot*, 11 December 1962, 17.

29. Temple, 126.

30. Ibid., 137.

*Chapter 15*

# Virginia Beach Today

T he city of Virginia Beach is the largest in the Commonwealth of Virginia with an estimated population of 425,605 in 1996. From 341,671 citizens in 1986,[1] the population has mushroomed by 25 percent, presenting Virginia Beach with opportunities as well as challenges.

## GOVERNMENT AND QUALITY OF LIFE

City leaders consider safe neighborhoods a major priority. Good neighborhoods and a low crime rate are two of the city's prime achievements.[2] A recent survey showed that nine out of ten citizens feel safe in their neighborhoods. Eighty-nine percent believe that Virginia Beach is a safe place to live. For seven years in a row, statistics from the U. S. Department of Justice show Virginia Beach with the lowest crime rate of cities with populations of 250,000 to 700,000.

According to Mayor Meyera Oberndorf, Virginia Beach has also been very successful in controlling expenditures. With 12.3 employees per 1,000 residents, Virginia Beach has one of the lowest city employee per capita ratios in the country for cities of comparable population. Efficiency and top quality service are main priorities for city employees.[3]

The City of Virginia Beach is organized under the council/manager form of government. The city manager is appointed by the eleven-member elected city council and acts as chief executive officer. The mayor is elected by the citizens of Virginia Beach and serves a four-year term. The city manager is responsible for implementing policies established by the council, while the mayor presides over council meetings and serves as spokesperson for the city. Meyera Oberndorf, the city's first directly elected mayor, was sworn into office on July 1, 1988.[4]

## EDUCATION

There has been a strong push to maintain the quality of education in Virginia Beach. The city's public school system currently consists of more than eighty schools[5] to accommodate a growing population. Regent University, Tidewater Community College, and Virginia Wesleyan College are also located in Virginia Beach, serving the needs of citizens who are interested in the pursuit of higher education. Construction of the Virginia Beach Higher Education Center near Tidewater Community College should be completed by 1999. It will be operated by Norfolk State University and Old Dominion University and will have an initial capacity for 7,000 students.[6]

The Virginia Beach Public Library system provides free access to accurate and current information and materials to all individuals.[7] It supports the educational needs of citizens with a system of area libraries, a central library, and special libraries for municipal reference, law, and outreach services.

## THE LAKE GASTON PIPELINE

A major challenge resulting from the population boom in Virginia Beach has been to find a dependable and economical source of drinking water. The City of Virginia Beach and various federal and state agencies have studied dozens of water supply alternatives. Some of these are waste-water reuse, seawater desalting, desalting of brackish groundwater, and building a pipeline to Lake Gaston, a reservoir located approximately 125 miles west of Virginia Beach. These studies have indicated that the "Lake Gaston Pipeline" is the most feasible project in terms of cost and environmental impact.[8]

Lake Gaston straddles the border between Virginia and North Carolina. In 1963 the Virginia Electric and Power Company (now Virginia Power) built the Lake Gaston Reservoir, which it still owns and operates. The Lake Gaston Water Supply Project involves the transfer of a maximum of 60 million gallons of water per day from Lake Gaston to southeastern Virginia, through seventy-six miles of sixty-inch diameter pipe. The plan calls for the pipe to be underground, with the exception of six river crossings. The project also includes building an intake and pump station on the Pea Hill Creek tributary of Lake Gaston.

Since its initiation in the early 1980s, the Lake Gaston pipeline project has met opposition on many fronts. There has been a great deal of controversy over the possible economic repercussions of the project. Some people have also been concerned that construction of the pipeline may have a negative impact on the environment.[9] The Lake Gaston project has been the subject of an intensive environmental review process. To date, the project has been the focus of ten federal reviews, none of which have indicated that the project would have any significant environmental impact.

An eleventh review is pending, with a decision expected by the end of 1996. All other federal, state, and local approvals have been obtained. Virginia Beach awarded construction contracts in December 1995, and as of June 1996, about one-third of the construction had been completed.[10]

In the meantime, the city continues a successful water conservation program and has formed the Hampton Roads Water Efficiency Team, known as HR WET, with fourteen other localities.[11] HR WET works with the media to educate citizens about the importance of "water efficient" habits.[12]

## INDUSTRY AND ECONOMY

The city of Virginia Beach is highly diversified in its economic base. Sectors of the economy include: agriculture; business and industry; construction and real estate; conventions; retail and wholesale trade; and tourism. Virginia Beach has one of the lowest tax rates in the state, as well as a higher median family income than the region's average.

Approximately 32 percent of the city's labor force is employed in the 7,500 retail and wholesale businesses located in Virginia Beach. About 32,000 acres in the city are under cultivation, resulting in a large economic impact on the part of the agricultural community. Annually, the convention industry grosses nearly $50 million in revenues.[13] Tourism generates more than $500 million each year and provides 12,000 full-time and 9,000 part-time jobs.[14]

The Resort Area Beautification Program, begun in 1987, provided a $10 million "facelift" to the Oceanfront area. The project included improvements to Atlantic Avenue and adjacent side streets, from the Rudee Loop to 42nd Street.[15] A recent survey revealed that repeat visitors to Virginia Beach appreciate the clean, attractive environment made possible by this beautification program.[16]

## THE MILITARY

The military is an important element of the economy in Virginia Beach. Four military bases are located in the city, providing jobs for approximately 34,000 armed services and civilian workers. Little Creek Naval Amphibious Base is the largest of its kind in the world and is the major base for the amphibious forces of the U. S. Atlantic Fleet. Fort Story, an army base established as an artillery post in 1917, is now used as a testing site for

**Corn Harvest** *above*
**Hog Farming** *below*
Hog farming and corn production are important elements of Virginia Beach agriculture.

Photos by Louis Cullipher, Agriculture Department, City of Virginia Beach

new ideas and equipment and is also a training site for all branches of the military. Dam Neck Fleet Combat Training Center, Atlantic, is used for training in combat direction and control systems.

Naval Air Station Oceana, one of only a few master jet bases of the United States Navy,[17] escaped closure by the United States Government in 1993 and again in 1995.[18] The Virginia Beach BRAC (Base Realignment and Closure) 1995 Committee, consisting of civic, military, and government leaders, was formed in an effort to keep Oceana open. Oceana currently remains the premier East Coast jet base for the United States Navy.[19]

## Recreation and Cultural Opportunities

Virginia Beach has excellent natural resources and climate.[20] A challenge presented by the city's growing population is maintaining the area's natural environment.[21] Adopted in October 1994, the Virginia Beach Outdoors Plan is the city's first attempt to create a system for the protection and management of its natural resources.[22]

Virginia Beach residents and visitors can enjoy the outdoors at numerous locations. First Landing/Seashore State Park on Shore Drive contains nearly 3,000 acres, with a campground and miles of nature trails. It is a habitat for 500 species of plants. False Cape State Park on Sandpiper Road is made up of maritime forests, dunes, and a campground. It is accessible by bicycle, foot, or boat. Back Bay National Wildlife Refuge, five miles north of False Cape, contains 5,000 acres of beach, woodland, and marsh.[23]

Approximately 10,000 acres within the city of Virginia Beach are used for recreational purposes. In addition to the larger parks mentioned above, there are over 160 city parks, 85 playgrounds, 210 tennis courts, 7 recreation centers, 9 public golf courses, and numerous picnic areas and campgrounds.[24]

One of the largest city parks, Mount Trashmore, has gained national recognition as a "modern marvel." The idea for Mount Trashmore was conceived in 1966 by Roland E. Dorer, who was then State Public Health Director of Insect and Rodent Control. Dorer believed that there must be a better way to get rid of solid waste than to bury or burn it. With the help of federal and state funds, Mount Trashmore was built using 640,000 tons of garbage.[25] It officially opened as a municipal park on October 5, 1974.[26] Located on Edwin Drive, the 165-acre[27] park offers playgrounds, picnic areas, and skateboarding facilities.[28] Kids Cove, a playground located at the base of Mount Trashmore, was built by community volunteers in 1993. Its design incorporates ideas from local children of the "perfect"

## Virginia Beach Scenic Waterway System

When formally opened in September 1986, it became the first locally developed comprehensive water trail system in the Commonwealth of Virginia. Visitors and residents can enjoy a variety of recreational activities on these scenic waterways.

Photo by Carole Arnold, Public Information Office, City of Virginia Beach

playground.[29] At sixty-eight feet, Mount Trashmore is one of the highest elevations in Virginia Beach.[30]

A second landfill, "Mount Trashmore II," was created in 1972. Located on Centerville Turnpike in Kempsville, it covers 353 acres and is more than twice as tall as the original Mount Trashmore.[31] After construction is completed, Mount Trashmore II will open to the public as City View Park.[32]

There is also much to be said for the city's cultural facilities. The theater at the Pavilion Convention Center seats 1,000 and hosts concerts and plays.[33] A 20,000-seat amphitheater, located on a 96-acre field near Princess Anne Park, provides an excellent setting for outdoor concerts.[34] The Virginia Marine Science Museum on General Booth Boulevard introduces visitors to the marine life of the Chesapeake Bay area, with hands-on exhibits and more than 100,000 gallons of aquaria. The Virginia Beach Center for the Arts, located on Parks Avenue, focuses on twentieth century art in America and includes international exhibits as well. The Old Coast Guard Station (formerly the Lifesaving Museum of Virginia), at 24th Street and Atlantic Avenue, specializes in Virginia shipwrecks and the history of the U. S. Lifesaving Service.[35]

**Pavilion Convention Center**
Conferences and cultural events in Virginia Beach are often held at the center.

Courtesy of the Virginia Beach Public Library

**Virginia Beach Amphitheater,** opened 1996

Photo by Carole Arnold, Public Information Office, City of Virginia Beach

A result of the population growth in Virginia Beach has been a dramatic increase in ethnic diversity. The 1990 federal census reported that an estimated 28,384 Virginia Beach residents were speaking a language other than English at home.[36] Population and housing statistics for 1990 also show that 83,833 residents in Virginia Beach were of Black, Asian, Pacific Islander, or Hispanic origin.[37] The largest Filipino-American community on the East Coast, numbering approximately 12,000, is located in Virginia Beach.[38]

The Minority Round Table of Hampton Roads, formed by representatives of the various ethnic groups in the area, began meeting in Virginia Beach in the early 1990s. Members of the Round Table hope to improve under-standing and cooperation between cultures and promote economic and political advancement for minorities.[39] In addition to the Minority Round Table, there are many other local clubs and organizations representing a variety of cultures.

History has proven that Virginia Beach is an innovative and resourceful city, dedicated to maintaining an excellent quality of life for its citizens. Owen Pickett, representative from Virginia's Second Congressional Dis-trict, states, "The City of Virginia Beach has the potential to become one of the most diversified, cosmopolitan, and lively cities in the eastern United States."[40] As Mayor Meyera Oberndorf says, "Virginia Beach is a city with a rich history and a bright future. We are all excited about the potential that exists in Virginia Beach. Through strategic planning, we've begun the process of making our vision a reality."[41]

From the beginning, Princess Anne County and Virginia Beach have experienced growth, development, and planning for the future. The his-tory of Virginia Beach does not end here but is for future generations to create. The sands of time will continue to shape *The Beach.*

# THE BEACH!

Courtesy of the Virginia Beach Visitor Information Center

## *Notes for Chapter 15*

1. City of Virginia Beach, Va. Department of Management and Budget. Memo. 24 June 1993.
2. Fagan Stackhouse, Director of Human Resources for the City of Virginia Beach, interview by staff of the Virginia Beach Public Library, questionnaire, Virginia Beach, Virginia, 28 September 1995, 4.
3. Meyera E. Oberndorf, "Civitan Club of Norfolk" (Speech presented to the Civitan Club of Norfolk, 29 August 1995), 3.
4. Public Information Office, *Your City Government: Virginia Beach*, n.d., n.p.
5. *MDR'S School Directory. Virginia* (Sheldon, Connecticut: Market Data Retrieval, Inc., 1994), VA-60.
6. Paul Clancy, "Plans Unveiled for Campus Shared by ODU, NSU at Beach," *Virginian-Pilot*, 11 May 1996, B1.
7. Virginia Beach Public Library. *Administrative Guidelines Manual*, September 1995. Virginia Beach, Virginia, 1- 4.
8. Thomas Leahy, Water Resources Engineer for Virginia Beach Department of Public Utilities, interview by staff of the Virginia Beach Public Library, Virginia Beach, Virginia, July 1996.
9. City of Virginia Beach, Va. Department of Public Utilities. Water Resources. *The Lake Gaston Water Supply Project, May 1995*. Virginia Beach, Virginia, 30-32.
10. Leahy, interview.
11. Meyera E. Oberndorf, Mayor of the City of Virginia Beach, interview by staff of the Virginia Beach Public Library, questionnaire, Virginia Beach, Virginia, 27 September 1995, 2.
12. Hampton Roads Water Efficiency Team, "Saving Today's Water for Tomorrow's Hampton Roads," information packet, n.d., n.p.
13. City of Virginia Beach, Va. Department of Economic Development. Information File for R. L. Polk. 1993.

14. Oberndorf, "Civitan Club of Norfolk," 2.

15. Ibid.

16. City of Virginia Beach, Va. Department of Convention and Visitor Development, telephone conversation with staff of the Virginia Beach Public Library, 12 February 1996.

17. City of Virginia Beach, Va. Department of Economic Development, Information file.

18. Dale Eisman, "Oceana's Future Open Thanks to Organized Local Effort," *Virginian-Pilot*, 24 July 1995, section 1, 1.

19. Oberndorf, "Civitan Club of Norfolk," 2.

20. Stackhouse, questionnaire, 2.

21. C. Oral Lambert Jr., Chief of Staff for the City of Virginia Beach, interview by staff of the Virginia Beach Public Library, questionnaire, Virginia Beach, Virginia, 29 September 1995, 1.

22. Oberndorf, "Civitan Club of Norfolk," 4.

23. City of Virginia Beach, Va,. Department of Convention and Visitors Bureau. *Virginia Beach Is Good. Clean. Fun.*, 1992. Virginia Beach, Virginia, 12.

24. City of Virginia Beach, Va. Department of Economic Development, Information file.

25. Ruby Jean Phillips, "Mountain of Trash," *Virginia Beach Beacon Visitors Guide*, 29 July 1973, n.p.

26. Jim Stiff, "Trashmore Municipal Park Opens Oct. 5," *The Beacon*, 4 October 1974, 21.

27. Marc Davis, "Mount Trashmore II: Garbage Hill 15 Stories High," *Virginian-Pilot and Ledger Star*, 19 October 1986, B 6.

28. City of Virginia Beach, Va. Department of Convention and Visitors Bureau, 12.

29. "Let the Play Begin," *Virginian-Pilot*, 17 May 1993, A 1.

30. City of Virginia Beach, Va. Department of Convention and Visitors Bureau, 12.

31. Davis, "Mount Trashmore II."

32. Pam Starr, "City View Park Official Name for High Trash Pile," *The Beacon*, 26 June 1994, 4

33. City of Virginia Beach, Va. Department of Economic Development, Information file.

34. Craig Shapiro, "Music in the Air," *Virginian-Pilot*, 15 May 1996, E 1.

35. City of Virginia Beach, Va. Department of Convention and Visitors Bureau, 13.

36. Bureau of the Census, *Selected Social Characteristics, Virginia Beach*, CPH-L-81 Table 1 (Washington, D.C., 1990).

37. Hampton Roads District Planning Commission, *Selected Population and Housing Characteristics: 1990, Virginia Beach City, Virginia*, Table 1 - Summary of STF 1A (Chesapeake, Virginia).

38. *Statistical Digest: Hampton Roads* (Richmond, Va.: Media General Business Communications, 1995) 14.

39. Charlise Lyles, "Area Minority Group Aims to Find and Fix Community Problems," *Virginian-Pilot and The Ledger-Star*, 24 August 1994, B 4.

40. Owen Pickett, U. S. Congressman for Virginia's Second Congressional District, interview by staff of the Virginia Beach Public Library, questionnaire, Virginia Beach, Virginia, 27 September 1995, 1.

41. Oberndorf, questionnaire, 2.

# A Survey of Historic Families

*In addition to the historic personalities discussed in Chapter 3, others became important to Princess Anne County and the city of Virginia Beach. They include:*

## CORNICK/CORNIX

Simon Cornick (Simond Cornix) received a certificate for 650 acres in 1653 for transporting thirteen persons to Virginia. Four of the thirteen were Jane, assumed to be his wife, and three children, Martha, William, and Thomas. The acreage was apparently not awarded until 1657, when William Cornick acquired the patent for the acreage due his father, Simon. The property was located south of Virginia Beach Boulevard, in an area known as Salisbury Plains. This area is now included in the property of NAS Oceana.[1]

William Cornick's wife, Elizabeth, was the daughter of John Martin and the sister of Adam Keeling's wife, Anne. William and Elizabeth's children were Joel (who inherited Salisbury Plains and married Elizabeth, the daughter of Henry Woodhouse), Elizabeth (the wife of Thomas Cannon), Barbara (who married Captain Francis Morse), and Martin, John, William, and Simon.[2]

## KEELING

Thomas Keeling came to Virginia as one of the 105 headrights of Adam Thorowgood's 1635 patent. In that same year, Keeling acquired 100 acres of land on Back River. He served as a vestryman in 1640. Upon his death he left six children. His eldest son, Adam (godson of Adam Thorowgood), married Anne Martin (sister of William Cornick's wife, Elizabeth). The Keelings, like the Woodhouses and Cornicks, were large landowners in the area south of London Bridge and Oceana.[3]

## LAMBERT

In 1635 Ensign Thomas Lambert patented the point of land on the Elizabeth River which still bears his name. By 1648 he had become Captain Lambert and received a grant for a tract in Lynnhaven Parish called Puggett's Neck on Little Creek. In 1652 he was a burgess for Lower Norfolk. He died in 1671, leaving his estate to his four daughters. In the same year, his four sons-in-law, George Fowler, Henry Snaile, Richard Drout, and John Weblin, filed a deed of partition for the Puggett's Neck property as co-heirs. As his wife's share, John Weblin received a tract of land which had the house, now known as the Weblin House, on it.[4]

## LAND

Francis Land (I) settled in Lower Norfolk County (later Princess Anne County) and had patented over 1,000 acres of land by the time of his death in the mid-1650s. Six generations of the Land family (all six heads of the household were named Francis) operated the plantation on a large tract of land, whose general location is known, but whose exact boundaries are not.[5]

The Land family raised tobacco as their cash crop during the first two generations. The 1760 inventory of Francis Thorowgood Land indicates that they had changed to wheat and oats production by the mid-eighteenth century. In addition, the Land family raised cattle, hogs, and sheep. An extensive vegetable garden probably helped to make the plantation self-sufficient.[6] The Land family members were active as church and government leaders.

## LAWSON

The Lawson family came to Virginia via Bermuda. Captain Thomas Lawson and his wife, Margaret Bray, had been shipwrecked in 1609 while aboard the *Seaventure*. Their son, Anthony, was born soon after their arrival at Jamestown. Anthony had two sons, George and Anthony (II). Educated in England Anthony (II) returned to Virginia from Ireland in 1668 and settled on the Eastern Branch of the Elizabeth River, adjoining the William Moseley and William Hancock properties.

Beginning with his first patent in 1673, Anthony (II) amassed extensive land holdings. He was, together with Captain William Robinson, one of the investors in Norfolk Town lots in 1680. Anthony (II) married Mary Gookin Moseley, daughter of Sarah Offley Thorowgood Gookin Yeardley and the widow of William Moseley (II).[7] Anthony Lawson (II) was one of the investors in New Town with William Moseley (II) and Edward Moseley (II). The fifty-one acres for the town were situated on the north side of the Eastern Branch of the Elizabeth River on property purchased from Simon Handcock (Hancock).[8]

## MOSELEY

William Moseley, his wife, Susannah, and their sons, William (II) and Arthur, were in Lower Norfolk County probably as early as 1649. In 1650 William (I) received a certificate for 150 acres due him for the transportation of eleven persons to Virginia. In 1652 he was granted a patent for land in Lynnhaven Parish. His manor, Rolleston, was located on the west side of the first creek east of Broad Creek and on the north side of the Eastern Branch of the Elizabeth River. Moseley became prominent in the county and served as a justice of its court. He died in 1655.

A deed William Moseley made to Colonel Francis Yeardley in 1652 and an earlier (1650) letter of his wife's addressed to Colonel Yeardley tell of the dire circumstances of the Moseleys upon their arrival in Virginia. Their lack of ready cash made it necessary to sell the family jewels for livestock. Colonel Francis Yeardley and his wife, Sarah Offley Thorowgood Gookin Yeardley, received one gold hat band, one gold and enamel buckle set with diamonds, one enameled jewel set with diamonds, and one enameled gold ring set with one diamond, one ruby, one "sapphyr," and one emerald. In return for these pieces, Colonel Yeardley gave the Moseleys two oxen, two steers, and five cows.[9]

William (I) and Susannah's son, Captain William Moseley (II), was a justice in 1662. He married Mary Gookin, daughter of Sarah Offley Thorowgood Gookin Yeardley and John Gookin. Arthur Moseley, William (I) and Susannah's other son, married Simon Hancock's (Handcock) daughter. He became one of the earliest lot owners in Norfolk.[10] Generations of Moseleys represented Princess Anne as justices, burgesses, and vestrymembers.

## MURRAY

David Murray settled on the south side of the Eastern Branch of the Elizabeth River about 1650. He received a grant of 300 acres.[11] Richard Murray, a great-grandson, operated a commercial flax business on the property. It was conveniently located for the local shipping industry and may have provided the flax used in ropes and sails. There were outbuildings for the business, including a flax-drying shed.  Early deeds refer to a flax pond on the Murray property.  Richard built gambrel-roofed brick houses for his three sons near the present intersection of Indian River Road and Military Highway.[12]

## SAUNDERS

Jonathan Saunders arrived in Princess Anne County in 1695 to be rector of Lynnhaven Parish.  He married Mary Bennett Ewell, the widow of Thomas Ewell.  Jonathan and Mary had two children, John and Mary. Following Jonathan's death, Mary Bennett Ewell Saunders married Maximillian Boush, a wealthy Norfolk merchant.  Together they had twelve additional children.

John's son Jonathan built Pembroke Manor in 1764.  He raised cattle, sheep, and hogs.[13]  Jonathan's son John inherited the manor in 1775. That same year he followed the lead of his guardian and brother-in-law, Jacob Ellegood, and answered Lord Dunmore's call to arms.  He returned to Princess Anne in 1780 as a member of the British Army to head the forces at Kemp's (or Kempe's) Landing.[14]

Following the end of the American Revolution, John Saunders requested restitution by the British government for possessions he had lost in Virginia.  These included "eight hundred acres of very good land with a large and valuable new brick dwelling house, an overseer's house, two kitchens, a barn and other out-houses, two apple orchards of more than seven hundred bearing trees. . . ."  Also included were furniture, books, crops, sheep, and twelve slaves who were listed by name.[15]  Following the American Revolution, John Saunders studied law in London, moved to New Brunswick, Canada, became First Justice of the Province, and fulfilled the potential he had shown as a young man in Princess Anne County.[16]

## WALKE

Thomas Walke arrived in Princess Anne County from Barbados in 1662.  He brought with him money and furniture.  His household goods included eighteen Russian leather chairs, a Spanish olivewood chest, a silver-headed cane, and two "silver hilted pistols."[17]  He remained a bachelor until 1689, when he married Mary, the daughter of Anthony Lawson. Their three children were Anthony, Thomas, and Mary.  When Thomas Walke (I) died in 1694/5,[18] the inventory of his estate listed large amounts of Spanish and other foreign coin.[19]  In a country where tobacco and tobacco warehouse receipts were used universally as money, the existence of coin was extremely unusual. In 1697 his executors purchased the land which was to become Anthony Walke's manor of Fairfield.[20] Generations of Walke descendants left a long history of activity in church and government affairs.

## WISHART/LOVETT/KEMP(E)

In 1673 James Wishart purchased property from William Richerson, who had previously acquired it from Adam Thorowgood (II). When James Wishart died in 1679/80, he left his plantation in Little Creek to his son William. Another son, James, inherited the property on which he, James, was residing. Two additional sons, Thomas and John, and two daughters, Joyce and Frances, were also mentioned in his will.[21] Thomas Wishard (Wishart), the youngest son of James (I), married Mary, daughter of James Kemp. James Kemp had married Ann, the widow of Lancaster Lovett (a church warden in Lynnhaven in 1650 and first of four generations of Lancaster Lovetts). The Kemp family established itself at the head of the Eastern Branch of the Elizabeth River, which soon became known as Kempe's (or Kemp's) Landing, now called Kempsville.[22]

## *Notes for Appendix I*

1. Sadie Scott Kellam and V. Hope Kellam, *Old Houses in Princess Anne Virginia* (Portsmouth,Va.: Printcraft, 1931), 105-106.
2. Ibid., 106-107.
3. Rogers Dey Whichard, *The History of Lower Tidewater Virginia*, vol.1 (New York: Lewis Historical Publishing Company, Inc., 1959), 277-278.
4. Whichard, vol.1, 279.
5. n.a.,untitled, from the Francis Land House, (typescript, rev. 7/90), unpaged.
6. Ibid., unpaged.
7. Whichard, vol.1, 279.
8. Florence Kimberly Turner, *Gateway to the New World: A History of Princess Anne County, Virginia 1607-1824* (Easley, S.C.: Southern Historical Press, 1984), 109.
9. Whichard, vol.1, 275.
10. Ibid., 275.
11. Turner, 116.
12. Louisa Venable Kyle, "Flax-Drying House Built in 1738 Is Reminder of Earliest Industry." 20 July 1952, part 5, 3.
13. Turner, 189.
14. Ibid., 192.
15. Ibid., 195-196.
16. Ibid., 197.
17. Ibid., 134.
18. Kellam and Kellam, 174-175.
19. Turner, 134.
20. Whichard, vol.1, 278.
21. Kellam and Kellam, 50.
22. Ibid., 205-206.

# A Survey of Historic Homes

*Because Virginia Beach grew from rural rather than urban roots, the historic houses which remain are tucked away among modern subdivisions and spread across the landscape of the city. There is no concentrated area, such as a historic district, with an accumulation of sites to be preserved. To insure preservation, each house must stand on its own merits and find its own supporters.* The Inventory of Historic Buildings and Sites by Age and Locations: As of July 1, 1989, *categorizes buildings and sites dating from the seventeenth through twentieth centuries. At the time of its publication, there were 320 historic buildings in the city. The following is a short list of some of these interesting properties.*

## BAYVILLE FARMS
4137 First Court Road

This 1822 house was built by Peter Singleton (II) on property that was in the original Adam Thorowgood land grant. He inherited the land through his mother Sukio[1] (Suzanna or Sukey)[2] Thorowgood. Peter Singleton (II) was a gambler and lost the house and land. James Garrison, the next owner, built a race track on the property and raised Arabian horses. One of them, Wagner, was so successful in local races that, in 1839, Garrison sent him to New Orleans and to Kentucky to race. He beat every horse he raced against, including the more renowned Grey Eagle.[3]

Additions to the house include two porches and a guest house built on the foundation of the old kitchen. The guest house chimney is built with bricks from the kitchen.[4] A 1936 book gives this twentieth-century view of the property:

*Standing on the lawn at "Bayville Manor" a beautiful picture*
*is presented. Rows of peonies, azaleas, tulip . . . bulbs and*
*shrubs grow in profusion . . . thousands of vari-colored*
*blooms - more than 1000 peonies . . . blend perfectly.*[5]

The tradition of raising prize livestock continued into the second half of the twentieth century. In 1964 the dairy at Bayville Farms won the Premier Breeder Trophy and awards for the best females in the Guernsey class of the National Dairy Congress.[6]

Part of the farm was sold in 1990 to developers who built Church Point on First Court Road. The farm, which had at one time included the entire peninsula bounded by Shore Drive and First Court Road, was converted to a golf course. The houses on the property were retained by the Burroughs, Tyler, and Stanton families.[7]

## BELL HOUSE
805 Oceana Boulevard

The only house of its type remaining in Virginia Beach, the Bell House is believed to have been built by Joshua James (II) about 1820. The house is typical of those built in the early part of the nineteenth century.[8] Joshua James (II) married Mary Dale Woodhouse in 1817. He wed Maria Capps in 1847, after the death of his first wife. Joshua James (II) died in 1860. Maria later married Alexander W. Bell whose name the house retains.

The house continued to change hands, owned by William Cooke, the Whitehursts, the Parkers, and others. In 1937 it was purchased by Charlie Cartwright who had the house wired for electricity. In 1942 A. T. Taylor bought the Bell House.[9] He restored the house and added to the property until it was about 1,000 acres.[10] The United States Navy purchased the property in 1952 to build Oceana Master Jet Base. The Bell House is used as the residence for the commanding officer of Naval Air Station Oceana.

## BROAD BAY MANOR
1710 Dey Cove Drive

Land was granted to Thomas Allen in 1655 on which a small house, one room with a loft above, was probably built in 1660. It had brick walls eighteen inches thick.[11] The house, twenty-four feet square, was incorporated into a much larger three-story house overlooking the water.[12] Later owners included Dr. Enoch Ferebee, his son and grandson, and Dr. John B. Dey.[13]

## DEWITT COTTAGE
12th Street and the Oceanfront

This cottage was built in 1895 by the first mayor of Virginia Beach, B. P. Holland. Bought by Cornelius DeWitt in 1909, it was occupied by the DeWitt family from that time until 1988, when the last of the DeWitt sisters moved to a retirement home.[14] The two-story house, which is on the Virginia Landmarks Register, has brick walls fourteen inches thick. It has twenty-two rooms, a basement, and an attic. The house is the only surviving example of the typical beach house erected in Virginia Beach during its first development period, 1863-1906.[15] In 1995, after remodeling, the DeWitt Cottage opened as the Atlantic Wildfowl Heritage Museum. There are ground floor exhibits of wildfowl and hunting memorabilia.[16]

## FAIRFIELD

The exact site of Fairfield is unknown, but it is believed that the entrance to the house was on Kempsville Road just south of Princess Anne Road. The property extended to the south and west from there. The house was built by Anthony Walke (II), probably between 1750 and 1770. After it burned, possibly in 1865,[17] his son the Reverend David Walke, who had lived there, moved to Pleasant Hall.[18] Fairfield was an "almost baronial establishment"[19] with liveried Black servants, blacksmiths, wagon-makers, saddlers, and tradesmen imported from England. It had the appearance of a village, with a number of houses and ships.[20] The last outbuilding remaining on the property was a kitchen or possibly a coachman's house, lodge, or office. It was severely damaged by vandals in the 1970s and was torn down.[21] The Fairfield name is perpetuated by a residential community and shopping area located on the site.

## FERRY FARM
Cheswick Lane

William Walke built a house at this site on land devised to him by his father, Anthony Walke. The present house was built on the same foundation in the early 1800s. It was on this property that a ferry was run in 1642 by Savill Gaskin.[22] The house has been the subject of title disputes. Future use, either as a residence or a museum, is being debated.[23]

# FRANK LLOYD WRIGHT HOUSE
320 51st Street

Designed by Frank Lloyd Wright in 1953 for Dr. and Mrs. Andrew B. Cooke, the house presents a conservative facade to the public. Away from public view, however, the architect let the "building erupt into full geometric bloom."[24] The crescent-shaped house with a curved wall of windows created quite a stir while it was being built. Many local builders and subcontractors were unenthusiastic about the design and did not bid on the work. They were more familiar with the square Georgian designs typical in this area. Enough adventurous contractors and subcontractors were found, however, and construction proceeded. One of the most difficult problems the builders had was the steady stream of curious visitors to the site.[25]

Completed in 1959, the house is made of sand colored bricks which were manufactured in Ohio and West Virginia. Frank Lloyd Wright also designed 90 percent of the furniture, the majority of which was made locally.[26]

# GREEN HILL
Lovetts Pond Road

The main house was built by Lancaster Lovett prior to 1738. A brick on the north wall is incised with the date 1738, which is thought to be the date that the roofline was raised and replaced, probably when it was owned by Lemuel Cornick. The Georgian house originally consisted of four rooms and a large cellar.[27]

Property ownership can be traced from its 1636 acquisition by Henry Southell (Southall or Southern) through the Purvine, Fulcher, Lovett, Keeling, Cornick, Godfrey, Lee, and Shull families.[28]

# GREENWICH
North side of Princess Anne Road and west of Kempsville Road

This site was the location of a plantation built by William Moseley (II),[29] who married Mary Gookin, daughter of Sarah Offley Thorowgood Gookin and John Gookin. Nothing remains to indicate the exact location of this property. The names of Rolleston and Greenwich, the Moseley plantations separated by a creek, are preserved in modern developments.

# KEELING HOUSE
1157 Adam Keeling Road

Thomas Keeling built this house sometime after 1680. It is a one-and-a-half story, five-bay, rectangular building and has a fine pitched "A" roof. The house is a good example of Flemish bond brickwork and has been restored to its former beauty. It has several notable features. The original woodwork includes matching cupboards on each side of the fireplace on the north wall. The house is one of only a handful of houses in Virginia which have a chevron pattern worked into the brickwork under the gables. The inverted chevron (created here in blue headers) was a distinctive late seventeenth century device.[30]

In 1683 Adam Keeling willed a 400-acre tract to his son Thomas. The property was located on the east side, near the mouth, of the Lynnhaven River. It is generally accepted that the house was built after the land was transferred.[31] The Keeling House is sometimes called "Ye Dudlies." This name is probably a modern misunderstanding of an old method of shorthand. To ease the strain of writing with quill pens, words were often abbreviated. A common abbreviation for "th" was called the Thorn and looked like a "Y." Therefore, the word "ye" would have been pronounced "the" and the word "yis" was "this."[32] When Adam Keeling referred to his house at "Ye Dudlies," he may have simply been referring to the house on the former Dudley property.[33] Owned by the Keelings until 1884, the house was later owned by the Averys, Consolvos, Whites, Syers, Manesses,[34] and Breedens.[35]

# LAWSON HALL
Lawson Hall Road

Built by Anthony Lawson in the eighteenth century, Lawson Hall was located in the Diamond Springs area. The property became noted for its extensive boxwood gardens. In the early 1900s a fire destroyed the house. Following the fire, a modern house was built on the site.[36] The Lawson name is perpetuated by the residential development Lawson Estates and nearby Lawson Lake, a dammed up branch of Little Creek.[37]

# MASURY HOUSE
515 Wilder Drive

In 1905 Dr. John Miller Masury, heir to a paint manufacturing fortune,[38] purchased 130 acres at the beach. The acreage, which extended from Crystal Lake for a distance of one-half mile to the shore, included 800 yards of ocean frontage. The house he built was completed in 1908[39] and was the only house between 31st Street and Cape Henry.[40]  It had twenty-five rooms, a ballroom, a pipe organ, an elevator, and a cedar boardwalk to the ocean.[41]  There were 3,000 square feet of verandahs and sun porches.[42]  Electric light was generated by a private electric plant, which also powered lights for the boardwalk, a beach cottage, and an electric train which ran on Atlantic Avenue.

The three-story building, also known as "The Castle," "Greystone," or "The Wilder Place," is built of gray stone imported from Scotland.  In the 1930s the house was the Crystal Club, a casino and nightclub.  It became a private residence again following World War II.[43]

## MURRAY HOUSES

At one time there were four Murray houses, each within walking distance of the others.  Two of the houses, located at the intersection of Indian River Road and Military Highway, were torn down to make room for a shopping center.[44]  The other two still exist, one on either side of King's Creek.

## RICHARD (or ISAAC) MURRAY HOUSE
3300 Harlie Court

This brick house on the west side of King's Creek has a brick near the top of the chimney etched "I.M. 1786."  The house is at least as old as the brick but probably older, as it is generally assumed to have been the first Murray family house and the site of their flax growing business.[45]  Like the Thomas Murray house, this house is also laid in Flemish bond.  There is a full basement with a fireplace.  The house contains much original woodwork.[46]

## THOMAS MURRAY HOUSE
425 Crestline Drive

The Thomas Murray house is a gambrel-roofed house built of Flemish bond brick.  Located on the east side of King's Creek, the house has a full basement with a fireplace.  There is a center hall on the first floor.  The house has wide pine floors, deep windows, and fine chimneys.[47]  It is believed to have been built in 1791 by Isaac Murray for his son Thomas.  Other than the installation of plumbing, electricity, and a kitchen, no modern additions have been made to this attractive house.[48]

## PEMBROKE MANOR
320 Constitution Drive

This brick mansion was built in 1764 by the grandson of Jonathan Saunders (who was rector of Lynnhaven Parish in 1695). At the time of the American Revolution, it was owned by the rector's great-grandson John Saunders, a Loyalist. The property escheated to the state and was bought by Captain Henry Kellam. The house is on both the Virginia Landmarks Register and the National Register of Historic Places.[49]

For many years, ownership alternated among those who proposed commercial usage and those who intended historical or residential usage. Now restored, Pembroke Manor is used as a pre-school.[50]

## PLEASANT HALL
5184 Princess Anne Road

Two bricks, set over a basement window of Pleasant Hall and inscribed with the date 1779 had long been a factor in attributing the building of the house to Peter Singleton (I) who owned it at that time. Research by Elizabeth Wingo, however, dates the construction to a period as much as a decade earlier. Using records from Virginia Beach, Richmond, and London, she identified that George Logan bought the property in 1763. Information written by George Logan's uncle, Robert Gilmour, indicated that the house was built in 1769 or 1770. Logan's widow stated in a loyalist publication of 1784 that Logan had built the house about seventeen years before.[51]

Pleasant Hall was the headquarters of Lord Dunmore following the skirmish at Kempsville. Because the owner, George Logan, sided with the British in the American Revolution, the property escheated to the state. The house, brick laid in a Flemish bond, is a fine example of Georgian architecture of the second period.[52] It has beautiful woodwork, including handsome wainscoting, elaborate cupboards and panels, and pilasters topped with Corinthian capitals.[53] So fine was the house that it was even admired by Lord Dunmore who is reported to have written, "I saw Mr. Logan's house and have never seen a better in Virginia."[54]

## ROLLESTON

Rolleston was built about 1650 by William Moseley. With the exception of one brief interval, it was owned by the Moseley family for 200 years. In 1860 the property was bought by former governor Henry A. Wise. He lived there for about two years but fled when the Union army occupied the area. By 1866 Rolleston was being used by the Freedmen's Bureau. It accommodated a school and residence for former slaves, with an enrollment of 130 children and adults. The house later burned[55] and is remembered now by modern place names.

## ROSE HALL
1101 Five Point Road

Jacob Ellegood built the original "Rose Hall" on this site in 1730. Many believe that the current house is similar to the frame house erected at that time. Jacob Ellegood, who was a prominent member of the community, a vestryman, and a colonel of the militia, sided with Lord Dunmore in 1775. After the Revolution he settled in New Brunswick, Canada. A family graveyard is located on the property.[56]

## TALLWOOD
1676 Kempsville Road

This house was built circa 1740 by Nathaniel Nicholas, whose grandfather arrived in Virginia in 1643. The property was owned by the Nicholas family until 1836 when it was sold to Jacob Hunter. The Hunters owned it until 1877 when it was again sold. The house is clapboard with brick at each end. The pine flooring and the stairway are original.[57]

Mrs. Lettie Gregory, who moved into the house in 1945, is credited with naming it Tallwood. The name was inspired by all of the trees which surround the house.[58]

## WEBLIN HOUSE
5588 Moore's Pond Road

Thomas Lambert was granted this land in 1648. John Weblin inherited it through his wife, who was Thomas Lambert's daughter. The house is believed to have been built prior to 1670. It is brick and has a large brick chimney just as the Thoroughgood house does.[59] One gable, chimney, and the rear of the house are of English bond, with the front of Flemish bond. The north gable and chimney are of a later period. Charred rafters indicate a partial burning and a later rebuilding. It is evident that the sharp roof has been altered to the gambrel roof style.[60]

## WOLFSNARE PLANTATION
513 West Plantation Road

This fine brick house was built in 1715 by Matthew Pallet (also spelled Pallette and Pallit). It is located on part of the Thomas Keeling grant.

The house is of Flemish bond and has outside chimneys at the east and west ends.[61]

The property and house remained in the Pallett family until 1835. In the following 122 years, it had nearly one dozen owners, including the Lovitts, Hunters, and Cornicks.[62] A property development company purchased it in 1957. Although the original plans were to tear it down, the house was used as a sales office and then sold as a residence.[63]

# *Notes for Appendix II*

1. City of Virginia Beach, Va. The Office of Research and Strategic Analysis. *City of Virginia Beach Inventory of Historic Buildings and Sites.* (Virginia Beach, Va.: City of Virginia Beach, 1990), 4-2.

2. Louisa Venable Kyle, "Bayville Survives, But Many Estates in Gay old Princess Anne are Gone," *Virginian-Pilot,* 24 May 1953, part 2, 5.

3. Louisa Venable Kyle, "Horse Racing in the Old South: How a Horse from Princess Anne County Became Champion," *Virginian-Pilot,* 15 August 1954, part 3, 5.

4. City of Virginia Beach, Va. The Office of Research and Strategic Analysis. March 1990, 4-2.

5. F. E. Turin, "The Making of a Great Port: Norfolk, Portsmouth, and Environs Today," in *Through the Years in Norfolk,* (Norfolk, Va.: n.p., 1936), 190.

6. Chris Weathersbee, "Bayville Takes Top Prizes at National Dairy Show," *Virginian-Pilot,* 30 October 1964, Beacon, 12.

7. Alex Marshall, "Bayville Farms Began in 1919 As Executive's Hobby," *Virginian-Pilot,* 17 June 1992, D5.

8. City of Virginia Beach, Va. Office of Research and Strategic Analysis. March 1990, 4-14.

9. Mary Hurst, "Commander's Residence Is Rich in History of Area," *Virginian-Pilot,* 14-15 January 1986, Beacon, 13.

10. City of Virginia Beach,Va. The Office of Research and Strategic Analysis. March 1990, 4-14.

11. Ibid. 4-13.

12. Louisa Venable Kyle, "Rich in Tradition, Broad Bay Manor Stands as a Reminder of More Spacious Days of Past," *Virginian-Pilot,* 22 August 1954, part 3, 3.

13. City of Virginia Beach,Va. The Office of Research and Strategic Analysis. March 1990, 4-13.

14. Marc Davis, "Old Cottage Has a Date with History," *Virginian-Pilot* 12 April 1988, D3.

15. City of Virginia Beach, Va. The Office of Research and Strategic Analysis. March 1990, 4-43.

16. Bill Reed, "Atlantic Wildfowl Heritage Museum Has Grand Opening Saturday in the Former DeWitt Cottage," *Virginian-Pilot,* 22 September 1995, *Beacon,* 8.

17. Sadie Scott Kellam and V. Hope Kellam, *Old Houses in Princess Anne Virginia* (Portsmouth,Va.: Printcraft, 1931), 167.

18. City of Virginia Beach, Va. The Office of Research and Strategic Analysis. March 1990, 5-3.

19. Kellam, 167.

20. Katherine Fontaine Syer, "The Town and City of Virginia Beach," in *The History of Lower Tidewater, Virginia,* vol. 2, ed. Rogers Dey Whichard (New York: Lewis Historical Publishing Company, Inc., 1959), 62.

21. Helen Crist, "Old Fairfield House to be Demolished," *The (Virginia Beach) Sun,* 17 February 1972, 1.

22. City of Virginia Beach, Va. The Office of Research and Strategic Analysis. March 1990, 4-2.

23. Greg Goldfarb, "There's a Cloud over the Title of 170-Year-Old House at the Beach," *Virginian-Pilot,* 21 February 1995, B1.

24. Sharon Young,"The Wright Angle," *Virginian-Pilot,* 14 September 1982, B1.

25. Jane Reif, "Frank Lloyd Wright Designs Unique Home for Virginia Beach," *Virginian-Pilot,* 25 October 1959, E1.

26. Sharon Young, B1.

27. City of Virginia Beach, Va. The Office of Research and Strategic Analysis. March 1990, 4-12.

28. Sadie Scott Kellam and V. Hope Kellam, *Title of Green Hill Farm Princess Anne County, Virginia,* 4 February 1932.

29. City of Virginia Beach, Va. The Office of Research and Strategic Analysis. March 1990, 5-1.

30. Ibid., 4-12.

31. Rogers Dey Whichard, *The History of Lower Tidewater Virginia*, vol.1 (New York: Lewis Historical Publishing Company, Inc., 1959), 278.

32. Paul E. Drake, *What Did They Mean by That?: A Dictionary of Historical Terms for Genealogists* (Bowie, Md.: Heritage Books, 1994), xi.

33. Nell Kraft, "Keeling House Is a Step into the 1600's," *Virginian-Pilot*, 8 September 1977, D1.

34. Louisa Venable Kyle, "Three Long Centuries Have Huffed and Puffed But They Haven't Blown 3 Brick Houses Down," *Virginian-Pilot,* 18 January 1953, part 2, 9.

35. Nell Kraft, "Keeling House Is a Step into 1600's," *Virginian-Pilot*, 8 September 1977, D1.

36. Sadie Scott Kellam and V. Hope Kellam, *Old Houses in Princess Anne Virginia* (Portsmouth,Va.: Printcraft, 1931), 219.

37. Rogers Dey Whichard, *The History of Lower Tidewater Virginia*, vol.1 (New York: Lewis Historical Publishing Company, Inc., 1959), 279.

38. Richard Cobb, "Mansion of Your Dreams Has a Real Price," *Virginian-Pilot*, 13 February 1977, section D, part 2, 15.

39. City of Virginia Beach, Va. The Office of Research and Strategic Analysis. March 1990, 4-15.

40. Cobb, 15.

41. City of Virginia Beach, Va. The Office of Research and Strategic Analysis. March 1990, 4-15.

42. Cobb, 15.

43. City of Virginia Beach, Va. The Office of Research and Strategic Analysis. March 1990, 4-15.

44. Mary Reid Barrow, "Studying the Fate of Family Farms," *Virginian-Pilot*, 7 October 1983, *Beacon*, 6.

45. City of Virginia Beach, Va. The Office of Research and Strategic Analysis. March 1990, 4-11.

46. Mary Reid Barrow, "Growth Makes a Casualty of History," *Virginian-Pilot*, 31 July 1983, *Beacon*, 6.

47. Louisa Venable Kyle, "Tuckers May Well Be Proud of the Home They Have Restored for Posterity to Enjoy," *Virginian-Pilot*, 6 December 1953, part 5, 4.

48. City of Virginia Beach, Va. The Office of Research and Strategic Analysis. March 1990, 4-10.

49. Ibid., 4-1.

50. Mary Reid Barrow, "Pembroke's Historic Halls Ring with Sounds of Children," *Virginian-Pilot*, 27 October 1993, *Beacon*, 2.

51. Helen Crist, "Studies Expand Home's Historic Value," *Virginian-Pilot*, 16 April 1982, *Beacon*, 4.

52. City of Virginia Beach, Va. The Office of Research and Strategic Analysis. March 1990, 4-10.

53. Janice Dool, "Pleasant Hall Harks To Era of Revolution," *Virginian-Pilot*, 25 May 1967, *Beacon*, 12.

54. Crist, "Studies Expand Home's Historic Value," 4.

55. Stephen S. Mansfield, *Princess Anne County and Virginia Beach: A Pictorial History* (Norfolk, Va.: The Donning Company/Publishers, 1989), 66-67.

56. City of Virginia Beach, Va. The Office of Research and Strategic Analysis. March 1990, 5-6.

57. Ibid., 4-10.

58. Helen Crist, "House Gets Name from 200-Year-Old trees." *Virginian-Pilot*, 28 March 1976, *Beacon*, 10.

59. City of Virginia Beach, Va.. The Office of Research and Strategic Analysis. *City of Virginia Beach Inventory of Historic Buildings and Sites*. March 1990, 4-1.

60. Kellam and Kellam, 36.

61. City of Virginia Beach, Va. The Office of Research and Strategic Analysis. March 1990, 4-14.

62. Louisa Venable Kyle, "Around Wolf Snare Creek Villages Now Are Growing Up Belatedly, to Fulfill a Three-Century-Old Colonial Vision," *Virginian-Pilot*, 2 August 1953, part 3, 7.

63. Carol Mather, "Wolf's Snare: 263 Years Old and Brimming with Vitality," *Virginian-Pilot*, 12 September 1978, A6.

# Selected Bibliography

Beverley, Robert. *The History and Present State of Virginia.* Chapel Hill, N.C.: University of North Carolina Press, 1947.

Bradford, Gershom. *The Mariner's Dictionary.* Barre, Mass.: Barre Publishers, 1972.

Cavanaugh, Michael A. *6th Virginia Infantry.* Lynchburg, Va.: H. E. Howard, Inc., 1988.

Champagne, Duane, ed. *The Native North American Almanac.* Detroit, Mich.: Gale Research, Inc., 1994.

City of Virginia Beach, Va. Department of Public Utilities. Water Resources. *The Lake Gaston Water Supply Project, May 1995.* Virginia Beach, Va.: City of Virginia Beach, 1995.

City of Virginia Beach, Va. The Office of Research and Strategic Analysis. *City of Virginia Beach Inventory of Historic Buildings and Sites. March 1990.* Virginia Beach, Va.: City of Virginia Beach, 1990.

Cragg, Dan. *Guide to Military Installations.* 4th ed. Mechanicsburg, Pa.: Stackpole Books, 1994.

Dabney, Virginius. *Virginia, the New Dominion.* Charlottesville, Va.: University Press of Virginia, 1971.

De Gast, Robert. *The Lighthouses of the Chesapeake.* Baltimore, Md.: The Johns Hopkins University Press, 1973.

Drake, Paul E. *What Did They Mean by That? : A Dictionary of Historical Terms for Genealogists.* Bowie, Md.: Heritage Books, 1994.

Dunn, Joseph W., Jr., and Barbara S. Lyle. *Virginia Beach "Wish You Were Here":a Postcard View of Days Gone By.* Norfolk, Va.: Donning Publishers, 1983.

Edwards, Andrew C., and Norman F. Barka. *The Archaeology of Upper Wolfsnare Virginia Beach, Virginia.* Williamsburg, Va.: The College of William and Mary, 1979.

Forrest, William S. *Historical and Descriptive Sketches of Norfolk and Vicinity: Including Portsmouth and the Adjacent Counties, During a Period of Two Hundred Years.* Philadelphia, Pa.: Lindsay and Blakiston, 1853, microfiche.

Fortier, John. *15th Virginia Cavalry.* Lynchburg, Va.: H. E. Howard, Inc., 1993.

Foss, William O. *The Norwegian Lady and the Wreck of the Dictator.* Norfolk, Va.: Donning Company/Publishers, Inc., 1977.

*Genealogies of Virginia Families from the Virginia Magazine of History and Biography.*
    Baltimore, Md.: Genealogical Publishing Co., Inc., 1981.

Harrell, Isaac S. *Loyalism in Virginia: Chapters in the Economic History of the Revolution.*
    Durham, N.C.: Duke University Press, 1926.

Hawks, Nigel. *Structures: The Way Things Are Built.* New York: Macmillan Publishing
    Co., 1990.

Heikkenen, Herman John. *Final Report: The Year of Construction of the Lynnhaven
    House as Derived by Key-year Dendrochronology Technique.* Blacksburg, Va.: The
    American Institute of Dendrochronology, 1982.

_____. *The Last Year of Tree Growth for Selected Timbers within the Francis Land House
    as Derived by Key-Year Dendrochronology.* Blacksburg, Va.: Dendrochronology, Inc.,
    1992.

Hening, William Waller, ed. *The Statutes at Large; Being a Collection of All the Laws of
    Virginia, from the First Session of the Legislature in the Year 1619;* reprint. Charlottesville,
    Va.: University Press of Virginia for the Jamestown Foundation of the Commonwealth
    of Virginia, 1969.

Information files and archives at Central Library. Virginia Beach, Va.: Department of Public
    Libraries.

James, Edward W., ed. *The Lower Norfolk County Virginia Antiquary.* New York: Peter
    Smith, 1951.

Jelks, Edward, ed. *Historical Dictionary of North American Archeology.* New York:
    Greenwood Press, 1988.

Jordan, James M., IV, and Frederick S. Jordan. *Virginia Beach: A Pictorial History.*
    Richmond, Va.: Hale Publishing, 1974.

Kellam, Sadie Scott, and V. Hope Kellam. *Old Houses in Princess Anne Virginia.*
    Portsmouth, Va.: Printcraft, 1931.

Kemp, Peter, ed. *The Oxford Companion to Ships and the Sea.* New York: Oxford
    University Press, 1976.

Mansfield, Stephen S. *Princess Anne County and Virginia Beach: A Pictorial History.*
    Norfolk, Va.: The Donning Company/Publishers, 1989.

Mason, George Carrington. *Colonial Churches of Tidewater Virginia.* Richmond, Va.:
    Whittet and Shepperson, 1945.

McCary, Ben C. *Indians in Seventeenth-Century Virginia.* Charlottesville, Va.: University
    Press of Virginia, 1957.

Meyer, Virginia M., and John Frederick Dorman, eds. *Adventurers of Purse and Person
    Virginia 1607-1624/5.* 3rd ed. Richmond, Va.: Dietz Press, Inc., 1987.

Palmer, William P., and H. W. Flourney. *Calendar of Virginia State Papers and Other
    Manuscripts.* Vol. 3. Richmond, Va.: James E. Goode, 1881, 1890.

Parramore, Thomas C., Peter C. Stewart, and Tommy L. Bogger. *Norfolk: The First
    Four Centuries.* Charlottesville, Va.: University Press of Virginia, 1994.

*Polk 1995 Virginia Beach, Virginia, City Directory.* Richmond, Va.: R. L. Polk, 1995.

Pouliot, Richard A., and Julie J. Pouliot. *Shipwrecks on the Virginia Coast and the Men
    of the United States Life-Saving Service.* Centreville, Md.: Tidewater Publishers,
    1986.

Rankin, Hugh F. *The Golden Age of Piracy.* Williamsburg, Va.: Colonial Williamsburg,
    1969.

Roberts, Nancy. *Blackbeard and Other Pirates of the Atlantic Coast*. Winston-Salem, N.C.: John F. Blair, Publisher, 1993.

Rountree, Helen. *Pocahontas's People: The Powhatan Indians of Virginia through Four Centuries*. Norman, Ok.: University of Oklahoma Press, 1990.

————. *The Powhatan Indians of Virginia: Their Traditional Culture*. Norman, Ok.: University of Oklahoma Press, 1989.

Sams, Conway Whittle. *The Conquest of Virginia: The Second Attempt*. Norfolk, Va.: Keyser-Doherty Printing Corp., 1929.

Schlegel, Marvin W. *Conscripted City: Norfolk in World War II*. Norfolk, Va.: Norfolk War History Commission, 1951.

Scott, Robert N. *The War of the Rebellion: A Compilation of the Official Records of the Union and Confederate Armies*. Washington, D.C.: Government Printing Office, 1889.

————. *The War of the Rebellion: A Compilation of the Official Records of the Union and Confederate Armies*. Washington, D.C.: Government Printing Office, 1890.

Shomette, Donald G. *Pirates on the Chesapeake: Being a True History of Pirates, Picaroons, and Raiders on Chesapeake Bay, 1610-1807*. Centreville, Md.: Tidewater Publishers, 1985.

Sifakis, Stewart. *Compendium of the Confederate Armies: Virginia*. New York: Facts on File, Inc., 1992.

Snow, Edward Rowe. *Famous Lighthouses of America*. New York: Dodd, Mead & Company, 1955.

Squires, W. H. T. *The Days of Yester-Year in Colony and Commonwealth: A Sketch Book of Virginia*. Portsmouth, Va.: Printcraft Press, Inc., 1928.

Stewart, William H. *History of Norfolk County, Virginia and Representative Citizens*. Chicago, Il.: Biographical Publishing Co., 1902.

Temple, David G. *Merger Politics: Local Government Consolidation in Tidewater Virginia*. Charlottesville, Va.: University Press of Virginia, 1972.

Turin, F. E. "The Making of a Great Port: Norfolk, Portsmouth, and Environs Today." In *Through the Years in Norfolk*. Norfolk, Va.: n.p., 1936.

Turner, Florence Kimberly. *Gateway to the New World: A History of Princess Anne County, Virginia 1607-1824*. Easley, S.C.: Southern Historical Press, 1984.

*Virginian-Pilot*. Norfolk, Va.

Waldman, Carl, and Alan Wexler. *Who Was Who in World Exploration*. New York: Facts on File, 1992.

Warriner, N. E. *A Register of Military Events in Virginia 1861-1865*. n.p.: Virginia Civil War Commission, 1959.

Whichard, Rogers Dey. *The History of Lower Tidewater Virginia*. New York: Lewis Historical Publishing Co., Inc., 1959.

White, Benjamin Dey. "Gleanings in the History of Princess Anne County." In *An Economic and Social Survey of Princess Anne County*, ed. E. E. Ferebee, and J. Pendleton Wilson, Jr. Charlottesville, Va.: Michie Company, 1924.

Williams, Lloyd Haynes. *Pirates of Colonial Virginia*. Richmond, Va.: Dietz Press, 1937.

# Index